Disrupting Pain and Activating The Soul

By: Ra'Mone Marquis

Thoughts And Affirmations To Feed The Soul

Disrupting Pain and Activating The Soul
Written by: Ra'Mone Marquis

Copyright © 2024 by Ra'Mone Marquis
Published by Tru Phoenix, LLC .

Table Of Contents

THANK YOU

Reneisha Byrd
Lauren Gomes
Shenitra Story
Shaniece & Jesse Caesar
Antoinett Brown
Keschmira Guerrier
Sharicka Lewis & Family
TeQuasha Carpenter
Brandon & Shelecia Bartley
Krystal Rogers
Tatiana & Thomas Dorvilus
Eartha Derricks
Andre Everette
Jonathan Moses
Rashard McCormack
Dr. Ajarvis Cobb
Sanford Barbee
TaQuanda Wade
Alicia Caesar
Zandra Russ
Shawnee Sumpter
Chimera & Eric Dunn
Tanisha Benjamin
Chaunelle Gomes
Yanick Ward
Jokera McNeil

Corine Lamont
Nicholas McGriff
Brittney Revere
Shanae Joyce-Stringer
Karen Kennedy
James Frye
Lenise Polydor

Dedication:

Amanda & Lawrence Fluellen (grandparents) – beyond grateful to have had you two to raise me. Along with giving me my foundation, and monumental unconditional love (R.I.P.)

Hattie Burnette (great-grandmother) –the brightest light and most amazing human being I've ever had the privilege to know and be loved by (R.I.P.)

Lamar Nelson (brother) – brother from another mother…taken away way too soon…an incredible and unforgettable impression you had and will always have on my life (R.I.P.)

Believe in yourself! Have faith in your abilities! Without a humble but reasonable confidence in your own powers, you cannot be successful or happy.

~Norman Vincent Peale

Letting go helps us to live in a more
peaceful state of mind and helps
restore our balance. It allows others to
be responsible for themselves and for
us to take our hands off situations
that do not belong to us. This frees us
from unnecessary stress.

~Melody Beattie

"Right actions in the future are the best apologies for bad actions in the past."

~Tyron Edwards

"Keep your dreams alive. Understand
to achieve anything requires faith and
belief in yourself, vision, hard work,
determination, and dedication.
Remember all things are possible for
those who believe."

~Gail Devers

"Hard times build determination and inner strength. Through them, we can also come to appreciate the uselessness of anger. Instead of getting angry, nurture a deep caring and respect for troublemakers because by creating such trying circumstances, they provide us with invaluable opportunities to practice tolerance and patience."

~Dalai Lama

"You gain strength, courage, and
confidence by every experience in
which you really stop to look fear in
the face. You can say to yourself, "I
lived through this horror. I can take
the next thing that comes along.'"

~Eleanor Roosevelt

In the same way that lightning always
finds a path to ground, feelings —
including those that are uncomfortable
and painful — always find a path to
expression. If we don't allow ourselves
to feel them, and as necessary talk
about them, if we avoid or suppress
our feelings…then they invariably
come out "sideways" in indirect forms
via our behavior.

You must ensure that you are internally safe and protected. The moment you are not properly taken care of, internally, it will bleed out into every aspect of your external.

When you don't take care of yourself,
you will always hurt someone else.

Get Your Fire Back

It happened and now it is done. It hurt you. You're broken. You're demotivated, angry, and in disbelief. Your trust was broken. Your expectations weren't met. Now what? You will be ok.

A lot of times when you've gone through so much, it's hard to believe. If you feel like things have been coming at you nonstop with no break, those thoughts and feelings are exponentially greater. God forbid you feel like you gotta suffer in silence or don't know who to turn to....God forbids you blaming yourself and not shaking that guilt. If you've pressed and pushed with no alleviation or progression, your faith is battered. Emotionally and mentally, most people are a blender of mess.

That doesn't have to define you. You may have to modify a few things. Your timeline may have to be extended. Don't let this defeat you. Don't let this destroy you. You are not done. I want you to get your fire back!

It will not be easy. It will not be quick. It will not be without a few obstacles. It will not be without a few uncomfortable moments. What it will be is worth it. Nothing is worth your self-esteem. Nothing is worth your peace of mind. Nothing is worth your growth or healing. Nothing is worth that joy being sustained. Nothing ain't worth that fire inside of you burning bright, big, and bold.

1. Stop carrying guilt for something that wasn't your fault.

2. Someone breaking your trust, heart, bond, etc...it was about them not you. Stop beating yourself up about it. Love isn't worth fighting for if you're the only one fighting for it.

3. It is ok to be guarded and cautious. In fact, I recommend it. However, make sure

that guard/wall you have up is protecting you not restricting you. You still need to live. Many will use their "guard/wall" to take the easy way out. You're not doing nothing but putting a band aid over something that needs surgery....you're not benefitting yourself at all.

4.   Take a self eval. If you messed up, if you had a part to play - forgive yourself. Take notes of where you went wrong and remember the signs so that next time you can check yourself and nip whatever in the bud. Growing can sometimes be painful, but so is staying the same.

5.   Stop giving people so many chances. Don't be stuck on stupid. When someone makes you more frustrated than calm, more stressed than relaxed; maybe it's time to find a new someone. Kick 'em out stage left!

6.   Stop doing the same thing expecting to get different results.

7.   Teach everyone in your life how to treat you and don't accept anything less. For your own mental health, block, delete, avoid, or ignore anyone who shows you they aren't meeting expectations. Do not let family be an exception!!!!

8.   The people who you spend most of your time with, do they help you achieve your goals or sit back and watch you while you achieve them? If they not helping what's their purpose? Goodbye!

9.   You can do bad by yourself. Don't let someone come into your life and make it worse. Every person you have some kind of relationship with; be it family, friends, associates, or by way of business...the relationship needs to enhance your life not stress it. If they stress it, let 'em go.

10.   Just because y'all share affiliations, bloodline, or history; you don't have to let them treat you any kind of way. Once again - teach people how to treat you and those that don't measure up - cut 'em off or deal with them from a distance.

11.   You need to be selfish with you at least once a week. Feed yourself internally, sleep, rest, whatever you want to do....but give yourself that no matter what.

12.   Hold yourself at the same level of reproach that you hold other people. Be for others what you expect them to be for you.

Get your fire back! Start off small and build each day. Overwhelming yourself will stunt your growth. Behind every smile is a story of numerous challenges and hardships that were overcome. The challenges around you are nothing compared to the determination within you. Remember, no one has ever achieved anything truly great without going through extreme adversity.

As you get your fire back. People, places, and things will not be the same. Some may say you're acting different. Dangit, you are because you're growing, and you want more for yourself. Those that matter will understand. So, some you will need to completely cut off or some just may need to wait. When I say wait, I mean this. Everyone can't go with you where God is taking you. Some will have to let you go on the journey without them and when you get there, you can reach back and get them. The people that are quick to walk away are the ones that never intended to stay.

Become addicted to constant and never-ending self-improvement. The best part about moving on is that you make room to give who's meant to come into your life the space to do so. Never forget you're in charge of your own happiness. Everything you want is just outside your comfort zone. The foundation of a strong self comes from small acts of daily discipline.

"Many of life's failures are people who did not realize how close they were to success when they gave up."

~Thomas Edison

Confidence Is Key

Confidence can be a powerful word. Confidence is a concept that involves not just an emotion but an important facet in individual's lives. When confidence is present, inside of a person, it exudes from the inside and can be contagious to anyone that may encounter it. Confidence is needed to take a small brick and turn it into a skyscraper. Confidence is needed to turn a store front business into a corporation. Confidence is needed to take a poor law student from Harvard and turn him into the President of the United States.

It is important for us as people to know that no matter what our goals are, confidence is our key to success. If you have been successful before, know that you will be successful again. Tell yourself, "I have succeeded in my past, and I know I will succeed in my future." Previous success is a huge component to one's self-confidence. One of the greatest resources that we can ever have is confidence. With confidence, we know that we can face any situation that comes our way. Without confidence, we will have struggles and hardships. If there is no confidence, anything that comes our way will pose as a threat.

When we lack in confidence, we acquire an increase in fear. Instead of facing something, we run from it, avoid it, and/or just procrastinate. In one's social life, without confidence, it will be in a poor state. We will start to question our desirability and disappear in the background or remain silent when we are in a group setting. In a person's social life, if they have no confidence, they will always have false perceptions when it comes to: missed invitations, missed phone calls or texts, or e-mails not responded to. This will cause a person to create in their mind, the thought that no one wants to include them, or no one likes them.

Confidence is essential to making it in life. It enables us to reach for our goals, try new things, and stand independently. It protects us from stress and equips us to face life's challenges. Confidence comes from believing in you. If you do not believe in yourself, you cannot expect someone else to believe in you. An individual's lack of confidence is just as obvious as one who has confidence. Believing means you unconditionally accept that you are both adequate and enticing. Acknowledging you are capable; means you are good enough, you are competent, and able to handle life's situations. Without a shadow of a doubt, confidence is truly one of the keys to success in any endeavor. The size of the endeavor is irrelevant.

Marci Fox, a licensed therapist, and motivational speaker, says: Believing you are capable and desirable, you are now free to face life's stresses calm and confident. It means whatever the task, no matter how overwhelming or small, you will handle it. The social situation doesn't matter. No matter how positive, no matter how negative or neutral, you will know nothing can negate that you are a desirable person. Confident people inspire confidence in others, such as: their audience, peers, bosses, customers, and friends. Gaining the confidence of others, I believe, is one of the key ways in which a self-confident person finds success. The good news is that self-confidence really can be learned and built on.

Your level of self-confidence can show in many ways, such as: your behavior, body language, how you speak, what you say, and so on. Look at the following comparisons of common confident behavior vs. behavior associated with low self-confidence. We gain a sense of self-efficacy when we see ourselves, and others like us, mastering skills and achieving goals that matter in those skill areas. This is the confidence that, if we learn and work hard in an area, we'll succeed. It's this type of

confidence that leads people to accept difficult
challenges and persist in the face of setbacks. The
good news is that becoming more confident is
readily achievable. Just have the focus and
determination to carry things through. What's even
better, is that the things you'll do to build your self-
confidence will also build success.

Confidence is not something that can be
learned like a set of rules. Confidence is a state of
mind. Positive thinking, practice, training,
knowledge, and talking to other people are all
useful ways to help improve or boost your
confidence levels. Confidence comes from feelings of
well-being, acceptance of your body and mind (self-
esteem), and belief in your own abilities, skills, and
experiences. Low-confidence can be a result of
many factors, including: fear of the unknown,
criticism, being unhappy with personal appearance
(self-esteem), feeling unprepared, poor time-
management, lack of knowledge and previous

failures. Confidence is not a static measure. Our confidence to perform roles and tasks can increase and decrease. Some days we may feel more confident than others.

Confidence and self-esteem are not the same thing, although they are often linked. Confidence is the term we use to describe how we feel about our ability to perform roles, functions, and tasks. Self-esteem is how we feel about ourselves, the way we look, the way we think....rather or not we feel worthy or valued. People with low self-esteem often also suffer from generally low confidence. While people with good self-esteem can also have low confidence. It is also perfectly possible for people with low self-esteem to be very confident in some areas. Knowing what to expect, and how and why things are done, will add to your awareness and usually make you feel more prepared and ultimately more confident. Learning and gaining knowledge can sometimes make us feel less confident about our abilities to perform roles and tasks. When this happens, we need to combine our knowledge with experience.

"Optimism is the faith that leads to achievement. Nothing can be done without hope and confidence."

~Helen Keller

To Thine Own Self Be True!

~Whitney Houston

Some people are just M&Ms –
Memories and Mistakes

My mistakes make me wiser. My failures make me stronger. My hardships make me thankful. My passion makes me unstoppable.

~Ralph Smart

I've made some mistakes I can't
change but I changed so I don't make
the same mistakes.

God when my lips no longer know
what to ask for in prayer, please hear
my heart.

Coming Back From Mistakes And Bad Decisions

It's too bad if circumstances were against you, or somebody you counted on failed you. Did you just have a bad day? This is life. Unfortunately, for many people this is normal. According to Justin Menkes' interesting book Better Under Pressure, truly great leaders don't blame others when things go wrong. They instead have a high "sense of agency". This is "the degree to which people attribute their circumstances and the outcomes they experience to being within their own control". We all make mistakes. Over the course of your professional life, you can count on making a few bad career choices. It comes with the territory. Still, those mistakes can really drag you down. And recovering from them is not a trivial matter, as I know all too well. There's nothing worse than failing by your own hand, your own hubris, or your own stupidity.

Jazz great Miles Davis once said, "When you hit a wrong note, it's the next note that makes it good or bad." To this day, I marvel at the wisdom behind that simple notion. If you just add a little self-confidence and courage, it's all you need to recover from even the worst blunders, career or otherwise. If you systematically reflect on mistakes, you will realize there are patterns in your performance that contribute to these errors. And once you realize that you are well on the way to fixing that pattern.

Reflect on the mistake that you made. Think about what caused it, and what you did that contributed to the situation. You can't learn anything from external factors, so forget about them. What can you do differently? This may be easier to do when some time has passed, especially if the mistake and its aftermath were particularly painful or embarrassing. Everything is temporary, including the aftermath of the mistake you are living with right now. Is there a lesson you can learn from this? If so, focus on that. This will help you avoid similar mistakes in the future. Plus who knows, perhaps someday you will look back and laugh on the situation.

When you've made a mistake and or done something that you regret; it is not quite beneficial to keep it all in. Don't try and be a quiet fixer. Mistakes often have side effects and pretending that it didn't happen is dangerous. Former Toyota chairman Katsuaki Watanabe stated, "Hidden problems are the ones that become serious threats eventually." You must apologize to everyone that is affected by your mistake. Make it a real apology, such as: "I'm sorry I caused __________. Or I'm sorry for________, because.......). Not something lame and self-protective, such as: "I wish it hadn't happened".

It does no good to dwell on your mistakes, which can lead to doubting your competence. "This type of thinking is actually self-destructive and only serves to hamper future effectiveness," says Liz Bywater, president of Bywater Consulting Group, a Philadelphia-based firm focused on optimizing organizational performance. "Remember: Failure is not in the falling down but in the staying down." You've apologized. You've taken your lumps. You've analyzed where you went wrong. Now, it's time to move on. Don't raise the topic of your mistake again.

Dwelling on your mistake will only leave you feeling depressed and helpless, which will not help you move forward. Give yourself permission to take your mind off it. Get lost in interesting articles on the Internet. Crank up your stereo and belt out words to your favorite song. Watch a favorite movie. Take deep breaths. Focus on the things you are most grateful for, whether they're your children, your house, or the food you eat. It is extremely difficult to be grateful for something and feel angry or down on yourself at the same time. Replace your self-pitying thoughts with ones of gratitude and feel the joy that come washing over you.

"Mistakes are like knives, that either serve us or cut us, as we grasp them by the blade or the handle."

~James Russell Lowell

Ctrl + Alt + Del
Control Yourself
Alter Your Thoughts
Delete Negativity

You gotta know the difference between
support and surveillance.

Happiness is not determined by what's happening inside you. Most people depend on others to gain happiness, but the truth is, it always comes from within.

~Adrian Corday

Change will not come if we wait for
some other person or some other time.
We are the ones we've been waiting for.
We are the change that we seek.

~Barack Obama

If you don't love yourself, you'll always
be chasing after people who don't love
you either.

~Many Hale

Aim, FOCUS, Thrive

We're stressed out and we're wired for distractions. That doesn't mean we have to live with them if they are disrupting our daily lives. In the office, we can set aside quiet places or even time periods to work when we need to focus and ensure that noises and music are kept to a minimum. At home we can set aside a space for working, so that when we are in that space our brains know it's time to work and not time to do the dishes or plan dinner.

Focus can only occur when we have said yes to one option and no to all other options. In other words, elimination is a prerequisite for focus. As Tim Ferriss says, "What you don't do determines what you can do." Of course, focus doesn't require a permanent no, but it does require a present no. You always have the option to do something else later, but in the present moment focus requires that you only do one thing. Focus is the key to productivity. Saying no to every other option unlocks your ability to accomplish the one thing that is left.

Instead of doing the difficult work of choosing one thing to focus on, we often convince ourselves that multitasking is a better option. This is ineffective. We can do two things at the same time. It is possible, for example, to watch TV while cooking dinner or to answer an email while talking on the phone. What is impossible, however, is concentrating on two tasks at once. You're either listening to the TV and the overflowing pot of pasta is background noise, or you're tending to the pot of pasta and the TV is background noise. During any single instant, you are concentrating on one or the other.

In their book, The Distracted Mind: Ancient Brains in a High-Tech World, Dr. Adam Gazzaley, a neuroscientist, and Dr. Larry Rosen, a psychologist, explains how our ability to pay attention works and what we can do to stay focused. In their book, they advise:

> "Although it may seem counterintuitive, we now appreciate that focusing and ignoring are not two sides of the same coin [...] it is not necessarily true that when you focus more on something, you automatically ignore everything else better. We have shown in our lab that different [brain] networks are engaged when we focus compared to when we ignore the same thing."

It's understandable that we are feeling more distracted than ever before, but there are tools we can use to combat distraction and keep moving forward. American Express has 9 ways for us to increase our focus and not get distracted. I found some of them very enlightening. Here they are:

1. Have a plan the night before

2. Turn off the distractions

3. Get comfortable

4. Unplug and play

5. Set smaller goals

6. Sleep

7. Use visual reminders

8. Reward yourself

9. Take a walk

MEASURE! MEASURE! MEASURE!

The trick is to realize that measuring is not a judgment about who you are, it's just feedback on where you are. Measure to discover, to find out, to understand. Measure to get to know yourself better. Measure to see if you're spending time on the things that are important to you. Measure because it will help you focus on the things that matter and ignore the things that don't.

Whatever avenue you choose to utilize, don't forget that anytime you find anything distracting you, all you must do is commit to just one thing. Initially, you don't even need to succeed.......you just need to get started!

"Pursue the things you love doing, and then do them so well that people can't take their eyes off you."

~Maya Angelou

A negative thinker sees a difficulty in
every opportunity. A positive thinker
sees an opportunity in every difficulty.

A dead battery can't jump a dead
battery! Get away from people who
can't charge your spirit when you need
a jump.

It's ok to forgive people and still deny
them access to you.

Sometimes you must eliminate to
elevate.

Inner You, Inner Who: Strength And Resilience

WE are stronger than WE think. WE are smarter than WE think. WE are better than WE think. WE are more deserving than WE think. If we look at the anatomy of inner strength, it's hard to outline what it exactly entails. One can see it in those who embody it. These people may not be very tall or physically fit, instead they might be slender and frail looking. This inner fortitude can take the form of compassion when dealing with an unruly child. Or even kind words spoken to a worried stranger.

All too often I hear people comment on how strong other people are, but do you know where inner strength comes from? It comes from hardship; it comes from living through tough times and dealing with difficulty. It comes from having to cope day to day and keep going regardless. Each obstacle that you overcome makes you that much stronger than you were before.

I have seen the results in my own life where practicing the action-steps of cultivating inner-strength, has greatly helped me deal with depression and lack of enthusiasm for life. As well as self-doubt and a sense of being overwhelmed when faced with obstacles on my path. Developing inner strength has helped save my life, in a variety of ways.

If you can tap into your inner strength, you might find that you are abler to forgive others. You'll know you are only in control of your own actions and that your happiness is not dependent on others. You might feel able to take back your power and change your story. Whilst inner strength is often tested in tragedy, it doesn't have to be. Renowned author, Tony Robbins, has 9 ways that

one can cultivate inner strength and resilience.
They are:

1. Use empowering rituals
2. Understand that your choices define your life
3. Raise your standards
4. Discover your purpose
5. Turn your "should" into "musts"
6. Let go of the past
7. Focus
8. Look to previous experiences
9. Set yourself up for success

"No matter how much falls on us, we keep plowing ahead. That's the only way to keep the roads clear."

Finding My Inner Strength

Many times, I felt like I have had nothing left to give. My heart, mind, and spirit need rest. I have wanted to bow out. Present one last curtain call. I've been on this rollercoaster ride for too long. No matter what, I am going to get off it. One way or another; I will get the rest that my heart, mind, and soul need. I have prayed, begged, and pleaded for it for far too long. How long does one have to die inside?

How can someone who is broken, be expected to pick up the broken pieces and move onward? When you call out multiple times...when you cry out multiple times....when you reach out multiple times....no response no movements....now what?

No significant other...no offspring...#1 motivation and motivator gone...#1 person I lived for or that gave me purpose is gone...I have never loved myself enough to where I felt like I am enough…I never loved myself enough where I felt like I was enough to be my own purpose for living. It was a state of emergency that I change that and change it quick. It is a flawed and uncomfortable journey at times, but it has also been exhilarating.

I remember in 2019, shortly after my life (in my opinion) fell apart, one of my fraternity brothers said something impactful to me: You must put one foot in front of the other and give yourself a chance! I didn't do that right away. I immediately gave in to the negative emotions. I immediately believed my world was broken and wouldn't be fixed. I immediately believed that I wouldn't make it. I immediately believed that I deserved all the bad that had happened. I immediately believed that there was no resolution. I had mentally and emotionally imprisoned myself. I allowed that internal imprisonment to consume every bit of me emotionally, mentally, and spiritually.

My journey with finding my inner strength first started with Acknowledgement & Awareness. I had to be completely honest with myself about all the areas that needed fixing. I had to acknowledge and be aware that I was doing nothing to fix what needed fixing. What I was doing to cope, was doing more harm than good. I wasn't suicidal at that moment, so that wasn't an option. What that did to me, was in a way force me to realize that I had no choice but to make it through this dark period... somehow. That's when Acceptance came about.

I had to accept that my life would never be the same. I had to accept that the one, who I once was dependent on internally, could no longer be my saving grace. I had to accept that I could no longer control my emotions and what they produced. I had to accept that I had to be submissive emotionally, mentally, and spiritually. I had to accept that it was me alone on this journey. No one could travel it for me, nor accompany me. I had to accept that relationships that I thought I needed or held dear, would become distant or completely removed. It was my responsibility and mine alone to do the necessary work to heal and grow. I did.......I have.

I then had to have Patience. The journey was not going to be short and there would be no expiration date. There were going to be hurdles and regression. There was going to be high levels of discomfort and vulnerability. There was going to be many times, where I wanted to give up and would be content with giving up. The test to my strength and readiness for real healing, would come in those moments.

Once I acknowledged, was aware, had acceptance, and forced myself to succumb to patience; next came restoration and reprogramming. I had to remember all the good things about me internally. I had to remember what I bring to the table. By being in a dark place for an extremely extended amount of time; my perspective, ideologies, beliefs were very tainted. It took a lot of reprogramming, some of which I'm still working on. My priorities shifted, my tolerance changed, how I moved changed, reactions and responses changed, and my expectations changed. All these changes were thrusted in a highly positive direction.

With finding inner strength came peace that I protect at all costs. Happiness beyond ever before, exists. Focus is strong and deep. Everything I do, anyone I'm around, anywhere I go – I am intentional. I make sure that one of my daily tasks, is to do the work to ensure that all of this is sustained. Self-love returned deeper than ever before. I was reintroduced to myself. Although, rough at times. I am enjoying getting to know the new me and what my new normal consists of.

Now listen! It isn't all peaches and cream. I have moments where I want to slip back into old habits. I have moments where I'm tired of pushing through stuff. Things pile up on top of one another, to test and try me. Most times I immediately say to myself, "Oh no I don't have no energy for this s**t again!" Fear comes...However, here's the situation.......my new self and my old self don't get along. They battle often. There is a renewed joy, passion, and fire that exists and gradually continues to grow. Due to this, the demotivated voice in the back of my head...isn't as dominant as it used to be. There is still some healing left for the heart to do. Although still emotionally, mentally, and spiritually fragile; I manage the internal seesaw, due to having altered my thought process and recognizing certain signs that prepares me to filter through my thoughts and emotions very efficiently...more efficiently than I have before.

As stated earlier, the journey is mine and no one can accompany or take the journey for me. What has been an asset, is my ability to open and let certain people in. These are individuals that have showed and proved. My circle or network may be smaller, but the quality is significantly bigger. Those individuals no longer in my life, helped add quality to my life by me removing them from it. I may be taking the journey alone, but I have a village that surrounds and uplifts me – and I'm more and more used to letting them play their part.

"Physical strength is measured by what we carry. Inner strength is measured by what we can bear."

~Anonymous

Inner Strength: Seek And Find

It protects and guides the mind, while feeding the soul. It can purify insecurities and fight against anything that threatens well-being. When tapped into, it is powerful and comforting....a nucleus and road map to one's better self and sustaining one's happier self. It has never left us, yet we have neglected it. We've abandoned and not tapped into it.

Sometimes, in certain circumstances, people display a great degree of inner strength that they didn't know they possessed. In difficult or dangerous situations many break down. Some display some kind of unexplainable power and help themselves and others. To make this power available to you at any time, you need to cultivate it. This requires training.

Sometimes we over or underestimate our strength. Just like written tests are used in school to check how well we have studied and understood a subject, hard knocks are used to test how strong we are in the face of life challenges. Painful life events can give you a double whammy. It'll be the initial pain. Followed by a lingering unresolved hurt that redefines who you are and robs you of your power.

Nothing gets you worked up like past regrets or worries about the future. You have no power over either. The more you ruminate on past experiences or obsess over what will happen, the more powerless you feel. Do you wish you hadn't said or done that in the past? Forgive yourself and start doing the right thing now. Tomorrow will take care of itself. Scratch that, tomorrow will be taken care of by what you do or focus on right now.

Strong inner strength gives us immense benefits. It gives us patience, a lot of it, which is always required due to us being very small entities. Inner strength, also called Atma Bala, is the strength of the soul. It is the core strength of a person, while mental strength is simply the strength of the mind.

If you are like me, you have plenty of voices inside your head at any given moment. These voices can represent a variety of reactions, thoughts, and emotions that you could utilize. When you take a moment and ponder how you want to react to a situation, you are tapping into your inner strength. Moreover, by practicing mindfulness meditation on a regular basis, you will improve your ability to hear your inner strength.

Author Kevin Daum came up with 7 ways to cultivate your inner strength. Those ways are:

1. Know who you are

2. Spend time in silence

3. Set a routine

4. Create the right circle

5. Gain control of your body

6. Give yourself a good home

7. Connect with the source of your power

If you feel that you've lost or forgotten your inner strength, www.powerofpositivity.com provides 15 ways you can regain that inner strength. Those ways are:

1. Seek out enjoyable hobbies and activities

2. Set small achievable goals for yourself

3. Find balance in life

4. Don't let negative emotions get the best of you

5. Choose to not let anything outside yourself dictate your emotions

6. Never stay in an unhappy situation

7. Make self-discovery a priority in the quest for inner strength

8. Avoid labeling yourself

9. Start meditating regularly

10. Eat a balanced diet

11. Move your body to build both outer and inner strength

12. Live compassionately

13. Never sacrifice your integrity

14. Let go of past pain

15. Don't overcomplicate life

"There are two ways of spreading light: to be the candle or the mirror that reflects it."

~Edith Wharton

Stress, Stress, Stress

Stress......where can I start??!!! Stress ain't nothing but the devil. Yes, that can seem cliché. Just like all of you, stress wears me out. Stress doesn't discriminate against age, race, financial status, or spiritual connectivity. No matter what walk of life, no matter how hard you work, no matter how much you try to do right...baby you cannot elude stress. Stress can kill you. Stress can cause health issues or if you have current health issues, stress can cause it to flare up. Trust me, I know. I am sure like many of us, we don't start off knowing how to adequately deal with stress. People turn to a variety of things and alternatives to deal with stress. Of course, stress affects people differently. Depending on the kind of person you are, determines how you deal with stress. One thing can happen to me and stress me out to the point where I feel like I'm losing my mind. Then the exact same thing can happen to someone else, and it barely affects them at all. I do feel that people who are well off financially have stress to deal with, but I feel they have less stress than someone who is working paycheck to paycheck.

How I deal with stress at 39, is not how I dealt with stress in my twenties or teens. For me, it depended on how bad I felt stress. I wouldn't eat. I'd be angry and snippy. My temper had a short fuse. In between, I'd be very moody. At times, I turned to sex or alcohol to temporarily take my mind from whatever it was that was stressing me. Yes, I was born and raised in the church. I would pray and all that kind of stuff. However, because my faith wasn't what it is now; I didn't feel that prayer helped me that much. For me, effective faith and prayer are intertwined. Both used to be very faulty with me. No matter what it was, I acted as if it was the end of the world. Small things stressed me out at the same level that major things did. For years, before I could get over one thing, something else happened. As stressful things piled up; I would feel more emotionally, physically, mentally, and spiritually broken and sometimes numb. In many situations, I took it out on other people.

Faith...God...Prayer...That's how I got better. I wasn't strong enough to improve on my own. Thus, prayer and God had to intervene. Certain people were put in my life who loved on me and fed encouragement into me. It allowed me to see myself in a different light. As I began to trust myself, I could open myself up and trust God more. This allowed me to have stronger faith in God, and that alone gave me a peace and happiness that I'd never experienced before. When stressful things occur, big or small, I'm already equipped to handle it. I don't start my day without reading my devotion. Now this was something my granny instilled in me since I was a child. The difference now is that my spiritual relationship has grown so much. When I read the bible, I'm understanding and internalizing what I'm reading.

Next, I pray. I don't just pray and tell God what I need and want. I have a conversation with him, like I would a friend or relative. This helps me stay on the right track. This helps me stay focused. I'm not perfect and don't strive to be. I strive for progression and that's what I expect to abundantly achieve. I also ensure that the people I spend most of my time with, are conducive to the kind of person I want to be. No matter how much I like someone or how close I am to them; I've learned to distance myself from them or cut them off if they aren't feeding the best of me. I want people around me who feeds the Ra'Mone that I am today and the Ra'Mone that is consistently evolving, not the Ra'Mone I use to be. There's a saying I saw on Facebook one time that said, "Surround yourself with the people who bring out the best in you not the stress in you." Or this other saying I love that says, "Stay around people who look more like your future than your past."

Faith, God, prayer, and working out has aided me in maintaining my positive maintenance of stressors. These are the things that helped me. Others may need therapy or medication, in conjunction to some of the things that helped me. Some folks may only need exercise. You may have some folks that can solely depend on prayer. The key is recognizing when stress is present and finding out what works best for you. Ensure your control and reaction of stress is beneficial to your growth and sanity.

The simple realization that you're in control of your life, is the foundation of stress management. Stress management is all about taking charge of your lifestyle, thoughts, emotions, and the way you deal with problems. Stress wreaks havoc on your emotional equilibrium, as well as your physical health. It narrows your ability to think clearly, function effectively, and enjoy life. Effective stress management, on the other hand, helps you break the hold stress has on your life. This aids you in being happier, healthier, and more productive. The goal is a balanced life. Have time for work, relationships, and relaxation. It will be an asset to you having the resilience to hold up under pressure and meet your challenges head on. Stress management starts with identifying the sources of stress in your life. This isn't as straightforward as it sounds. While it's easy to identify major stressors, such as: changing jobs, moving, or a going through a divorce. Pinpointing the sources of chronic stress can be more complicated.

Many people cope with stress in ways that compound the problem. Some of the bad ways to deal with stress are:

- Smoking
- Using pills or drugs to relax
- Drinking too much

- Withdrawing from friends, family, and activities
- Binging on junk or comfort food
- Procrastinating
- Zoning out for hours looking at your phone
- Filling up every minute of the day to avoid facing problems
- Sleeping too much
- Taking out your stress on others

A variety of situations are what brings predictable levels of stress, such as: meetings, family gatherings, work project, court, etc. When the predictable or unpredictable stressors arise, I came across something known as the 4 A's that can help you better control the levels of stress that may come your way:

- Avoid – avoid people who stress you out, learn to say no, take control of your environment, and pare down your to do list

- Alter – create a balanced schedule, express your feelings instead of bottling them up, and be willing to compromise
- Adapt – adjust your attitude, practice gratitude, and reframe problems
- Accept – look for the upside, share your feelings, learn to forgive, and don't try to control the uncontrollable

A new study out of Ohio State University and published in the Journal Proceedings of the National Academy of Sciences, found that dealing with persistent and long-term stress (like that from a toxic boss or from caring for an elderly parent) can actually change your genes; leading to an increase in inflammation that can bring on a variety of health issues. Research indicates that the vitamin D boost from sunlight may elevate your levels of feel-good serotonin. Take in the sights, sounds, and smells around you; this redirects your focus from your worries, says Kathleen Hall, a

health educator and the founder and CEO of
the Stress Institute. Research from the University of
California, Los Angeles shows your body produces
less of the stress hormone cortisol when engaging
in guided imagery. There are plenty of books and
articles written on the subject if you need help
getting started. The most important thing is to find
a comforting and calming image that works for you.
While studying brain activity, the National Institute
of Health researchers found subjects who showed
more gratitude had higher levels of activity in the
hypothalamus. This is a part of the brain that has a
huge influence on our stress levels. Gratefulness
also activated the regions associated with
dopamine, one of those feel-good neurotransmitters.
To reap these stress-reducing benefits, write down
your feelings of gratitude daily in a journal. Another
option is to send little notes to friends or family
letting them know how much you appreciate them.

Through research and my own alternatives that have benefitted me, I found 5 ways that I feel could really benefit you with maintaining or alleviating levels of stress:

- Lie face down on the floor and begin breathing deeply and slowly, with your hands resting under your face. Do this for five minutes.
- Avoid using caffeine, alcohol, nicotine, junk food, binge eating, and other drugs as your primary means for coping with stress. While they can be helpful occasionally, using them as your only or usual method will result in longer-term problems. Included in this, would be such issues as weight problems or alcoholism.
- Make time for music, art, or other hobbies that help relax and distract you.
- Learn to just say, "No" occasionally. It won't hurt other people's feelings as much as you

think. This is simply a method to be more assertive in your own life and to better help you meet your own needs.

Stress acts as an accelerator: it will push you either forward or backward, but you choose which direction.

~Chelsea Erieau

It's ok to be a glowstick. Sometimes we
must break before we shine.

~Jadah Sellner

You got to stop telling bad spirits good news.

Don't let nobody who ain't been in your shoes, tell you how to tie your laces.

Having a vision for what you want is
not enough...vision without execution
is hallucination.

Grief

Grief is the process an individual goes through after losing a significant person or element from their life. While grief is usually associated with the loss of human life, that is not the only cause of grief. Any significant loss can be emotionally difficult and disruptive for an individual, and it can also cause complicated grief in some people.

There are a few common causes of grief, such as:

- Death of a loved one: Losing a person you are close to is the most recognized cause of grief. Coping with the death of a loved one in the family, is one of the most common human experiences.

- Suicide loss: When a person loses someone to suicide, grief can be more challenging and complicated to process.

- Divorce: While divorce is not the same as a person's death, it can cause both parties to grieve. Divorce represents a complex change that can impact many parts of life.

- Loss of job: The loss of a job can be a devastating and life-changing event. Job loss grief reflects the lack of financial security and can affect personal identity.

- Death of a pet: For some people, the death of a pet can be as significant as the loss of a human life. This is especially true when grieving the loss of pets who are viewed as family members.

The normal reactions of grief overlap several symptoms of depression and anxiety disorders. Crying, low mood, disrupted sleep, and loss of

appetite are common during the early stages
of grief. Anxiety and depression disorders show
similar symptoms for several weeks at a time.

According to an article from Psychiatric Times,
40% of grievers meet the criteria for major
depression one month after their loss, and 24% still
meet the criteria after two months. Due to these
similarities, a bereaved person cannot be diagnosed
with depression until two months have passed
since their loss. There are real, physical symptoms,
and side effects that come with intense grief: 65% of
Americans going through intense grieving
experience some sort of physical ailment, or a
combination of multiple ones.

I remember being a little kid when one of my
idols died, Tupac Shakur. I was too young to be
listening to his music, but I loved the hell out of it. I
looked up to him and respected him for so much,
i.e. lyrics, intellect, personality, and just him being
a pure multi-faceted entertainer. The same aspects

and then some, connected me to Whitney Houston. Of course, since I didn't know these individuals personally, I experienced brief sadness not grief.

My first experience with grief, was when my great-grandmother died during my 10th grade year. She was an amazing woman. I couldn't be around her enough. She loved the hell out of me. I was her favorite. Her death hit our family hard. For me, at a very young age, my heart got used to losing people and things that I loved. Due to being young and resilient, I remember being very sad and had a moment where I broke down. However, I just wanted to do my best to be there for my granny, because losing her mom was extremely hard for her. She carried some levels of guilt, which I later learned is part of the grieving process. They were so close, and I idolized the love they had as parent and child.

I lost someone who I felt was one of the few people, in not just my family but in my life, that loved me. I was constantly provided loving affirmations. When you feel like a lot of people who should love you do not, the few people that do – it does something to you when you lose them. I was raised by my maternal grandmother, and we supported the hell out of each other. When her mom died, for me I wasn't a bad kid; I had a plethora of internal issues that at times manifested inaccurately in some of my words and behaviors. I wanted to find my own ways to deal as to not add any stressors to her already full plate.

Throughout my childhood and my 20s, I attended a lot of funerals. When I say a lot...I mean a lot. Due to a lot of things, I'd been through, I'd become very successful at turning my emotions on and off. Although experiencing moments of sadness, being this way prohibited myself from experiencing certain emotions. These funerals were that of people who were relatives, classmates, close friends, and friends of the family. There was one clear reason why there was no actual experience of a grief process. Other than my great-grandmother and a cousin, none of these individuals had a large enough presence in my life. Thus, my emotional and mental facets never escalated beyond brief bouts of sadness. The one to two days after, I'd just move on with my life.

It was always a gift, and in my thirties, I learned it was also a curse. For me to suppress and control my emotions so swiftly and deeply, as I always could. HOWEVER….LORD HAVE MERCY…when my grandmother died on June 5, 2019. Every gift, technique, and positive coping mechanism that I'd internalized – had went out the window. My entire world fell apart and that's just putting it mildly! Honestly, I still haven't fully recovered.

My granny, Amanda Burnette Fluellen, was my heart and my everything. Neither one of us could explain it, but we've had a very special connection since I was born. She loved me unconditionally. She was always my #1 supporter and educator. She introduced me to God and fed that relationship daily. Many people, especially in my family, probably wonder why I praised and upheld her so much? Why, no matter anything done or said, was she always #1? Why was she significantly more important to me than anyone else? She did something that NO ONE else on this earth ever did.......she fed and protected my heart.

My granny was strict, hard, and played no games. She was not to be toiled with. I soaked all of it up. No matter what life threw my way, I always knew I was going to be ok. Why? I knew she was somewhere praying for me daily! We had the best conversations that always fed my soul and mind. Although, some of her lectures would sting – she knew how to provide that sting in a way that allowed me to never forget how much she loved me. We are so much alike it's ridiculous LOL. I was one of the luckiest people in the world, because she loved me...because she raised me. We had a level of trust, comfort, and protection that she never had with anyone else. I'm aware that I'll never have that again with anyone else.

When everyone who was supposed to love me in turn pained me, betrayed me, and neglected me. She lifted me up every time. She wiped every tear aways...literally. Her and my grandfather rescued me from abuse, abandonment, and neglect as a child. Up until the day she died, she hugged me in a way that always made life's troubles and hell seem conquerable. When she died a huge part of me died too. Yes, biologically she was my maternal grandmother, she raised me. So, the foundation of our connection consisted of that of a mother and child. This is no way diminishes my biological mom. I know she loves me, and I'll always love her back.

My granny was a big part of my purpose, motivation, passion, and everything that was great about life. She instilled in me the concept and gift of being in control of myself internally (emotionally and mentally), and always remembering that I am strong and can make it through anything. Many times, she had more confidence in myself than I did. My grief and trauma unfortunately did not stop there.

One year after my grandmother died, I lost a brother to gun violence. Although my grandmother's death was not expected, it was easier to understand. Years prior she had a heart attack. I knew her health wasn't 100%. However, to lose someone due to them being murdered; that is a different type of pain and trauma. Six months later I lost the ONLY relative on my paternal side, that I had a relationship with. It as an aunt. Never knew she had health issues. I knew some time had passed since we spoke, and I didn't get any response to any of my calls or texts. I found out about her death by Facebook, while on vacation with friends in the Bahamas. With each one of these deaths, I emotionally, mentally, and spiritually got worse. Nothing I tried could help me heal. Just about anything you could think of, I tried. It masked it all but didn't give me any healing. I hid behind my podcast, my books, my blog, my foundation, my personality, and my job. Then September 2022, nine months after losing my aunt, the last of my parental unit died...my grandfather. Biologically that was his title. In life he was my dad. That tipped me over the edge. From 2019 to today (2023), I have had six people close to me die. I regressed from any kind of progression I had mentally, emotionally, and spiritually. I had suicidal ideations for the first time in ten years. Once in February of 2023 and twice in March of 2023. Only my therapist knew. Unlike ten years prior, I did not attempt anything that my ideations were leading me toward.

Regarding the grief process, I diminished the seriousness and truth of the warning people gave me that stated: I have to let the emotions out. I won't be able to control the emotions. The grief process lasts a long time. Grief never goes away; you just learn to manage it better. I set myself up big time!

My moods were like a seesaw all day and every day. I could be happy one minute and as quick as I blink my eye, I'm crying. Within a span of an hour, I could experience five different emotions. When each one hits me, it's like I'm getting hit by a wave. I literally had zero control. The more I tried to control the emotions, the worse I got. When I allowed myself to just ride the wave, it would give me some temporary relief. My appetite fluctuated, but never became a concern to me. I lost all passion and joy for life. As I'm writing this, I still have some healing to do in this department.

The need to isolate was very big. I knew early on how important it was going to be to protect my peace. Thus, I was very picky with whom I spent time with. I also had a different perspective of the folk in my life. I realized who needed to be removed from my life versus the ones who served my life purpose, emotionally and mentally. There is not one person that I cut out of my life, that I regret. With there already being a plethora of negative stresses in my life, it made the grief process a lot worse.

2019 was already the worst year of my life and my granny's death made it worse. My life continued to get worse since then. Spiritually, I was broken and that contributed to internal spiritual warfare. I fed myself spiritually constantly. I was mentally and emotionally numb and flat out did not care about anything - including myself. I continued to go to work. I continued seeing my therapist that I'd been seeing since 2016. I ended up working with a different therapist in 2022. Before I could have any progress something else painful would happen. I continued to experience trauma after trauma with no break. It was like I was fighting an uphill battle, but nothing I did moved me anywhere upward.

Due to all the stressors and pain I've had to deal with, beyond the deaths; I am a strong believer in that this was a defining factor in me having such a difficult time navigating through life. So far what has assisted me with regaining sanity and progression with my healing, has been therapy and no isolation. Allowing myself to interact with people I trusted. Also feeding myself spiritually every day and working on patience with God. Having faith in God or a higher power doesn't mean things will change overnight. If anything, the closer I've felt to God – the longer it has taken me to heal or have any progression. This made it more difficult to remain a spiritual person. I very much have been heavily under construction spiritually. I have been consumed by no faith or hope in God, myself, life, and anyone or anything.

To this day I still struggle and fight with this, but that's a topic of another day. My relationship with God has been the most beneficial one, but also the most stressful and pained one. Then there's self-care. Rather listening to music, working out, pampering myself; self-care is vastly important to the health of my mind, body, and spirit. By sustaining all these things, it has helped me to ride the waves better. Although a rollercoaster ride, I so desperately want to get off of; it has significantly helped me brace myself better through all of the dips, turns, and tricks of life.

To give ourselves a higher change of healing from and moving through grief, we must be aware of the five stages of grief. Great Lakes Psychology Group discusses these stages in a very relatable and simple way. They are:

1. Denial and Isolation - When we lose someone or something important to us, it is

natural to reject the idea that it could be true. In turn, we may isolate ourselves to avoid reminders of the truth.

2. Anger - When it is no longer possible to live in denial, it is common to become frustrated and angry.

3. Bargaining - We might somehow seek to change the circumstances of the situation causing our grief. Bargaining may be an attempt to regain a sense of control as a defense against helplessness.

4. Depression - In this stage, we feel the full weight of our sadness over the loss. The grieving person may describe feeling deep sorrow, anguish, and mental pain.

5. Acceptance - many grief experts say that grief can continue for a lifetime after a major loss, and coping with the loss only becomes easier over time. Waves of grief can be triggered by reminders of the loss,

long after it has happened and long after the person has "accepted" it.

It is important to know that, while dealing with grief, you can move through any of the five stages multiple times. Grief may possibly seem insurmountable when it first attacks your life. However, there are ways to cope with it. There are seven steps that I feel are essential and effective.

1. Give yourself permission to feel - Be sure to recognize the need to grieve and let it run its natural course. Your emotional health will be better served if you face your grief.
2. Write a letter to the deceased loved one. Writing a message about your emotions can be cathartic and aid with coping.
3. Journal about positive memories - a journal about positive memories and experiences will help you focus on the good times.

4. Talk to someone - People may feel safer shutting everyone else out during their time of grief. Resist that urge and find a confidante to share with.

5. Be aware that grief affects everyone - Grief is not age-specific or limited to certain populations. Everyone has their own unique form of grieving. There is no instruction manual on how to grieve.

6. Give others a supportive ear - It's still important to support your loved ones during their grieving process. Be there to listen and comfort them. Let them work through the process and answer their questions directly as they arise.

7. Prepare for recurring grief – (this one gets me every time) Holidays, birthdays and other events can spark grief — even years after a loss. Recognize these triggers and prepare to handle the grief as needed.

"Grief never ends...But it changes. It's a passage, not a place to stay. Grief is not a sign of weakness, nor a lack of faith...It is the price of love!"

Release Some Tension

In contrast to the times, when people like to open up and share their feelings with others, there are times when people prefer to hide their feelings and keep others from knowing how they really feel. This can be for moral or personal reasons, such as: not wanting to hurt others, being uncomfortable with expressing themselves, and not wanting other people feeling sorry for them. One of the biggest reasons, is that people are often afraid of the consequences. They don't want to be vulnerable and prefer not sharing their intimate details about oneself with others. Almost everyone experiences feelings of being hurt, humiliated, threatened, angry, sad, or used. When people prefer not to express themselves, they put on a fake smile and hide their true feeling. This occurs when they sense that they are being viewed.

Often people start tending to hide their feelings when it comes to concerns of other people's feelings. Obviously, for people to be liked, and bring out a good impression, they will want to avoid the state of hurting others. They would also prevent any unpleasant situations. Almost everyone has been in situations when they were invited for a dinner by their friends or relatives. People usually tend to prefer food that is familiar rather than exotic. Even if the food that the relative or a friend prepared did not seem very tasty, people would not usually admit it. Instead, in order not to hurt the person's feelings; people would want to be polite, thank the person, and tell them that the dinner was wonderful. Even though that is not how they really felt about it.

All of us can feel happiness, fear, sadness, disgust, surprise, or anger at any time. What does all these words have in common? They are so-called six basic emotions and are specific reactions to events related to biochemical (internal) and environmental (external) influences. There are more than a half of a thousand different words in English that can describe every emotion, and we have over 40 muscles in our face to express them.

We feel emotions by our brain, and it is really difficult for scientists to give a single accurate definition for this process. Experts say that emotions are our mental state along with facial expressions, actions, or physical changes. They are related to our mood but differ from it. As they are short lived feelings with a clear object and mood is a more general feeling and lasts longer. For example, one can be happy about something or angry with somebody - this is their emotion. Another one can have a general feeling of pleasure, anxiety, or sadness - this is his mood.

It is easy for us to feel emotions, but it is quite complicated to study them. According to many researchers in this field, emotions have components of two types: physical and mental. Additionally, they consist of body responses, expressive behavior, and subjective feelings. An extremely important aspect of self-disclosure is the sharing of feelings. We all experience feelings such as happiness at an unexpected gift, sadness about the breakup of a relationship, or anger when we believe we have been taken advantage of. The question is whether to disclose such feelings, and if so, how. Self-disclosure of feelings usually will be most successful not when feelings are withheld or displayed, but when they are described.

Expressing feelings, dealing with problems, and moving on can be a difficult challenge. This is particularly true in high stress environments. Aside from general responsibilities, this is further aggravated by the downsizing, restructuring, and multi-tasking that is occurring in many of today's businesses. The occasional expression of emotional behavior is not necessarily a negative thing. Except when it becomes so amplified or recurs so often that it prevents people from dealing rationally and productively, with those around them. An expression of emotion may be an important cue that something is interfering with an employee's ability to work effectively. One cannot always control what happens, but one can learn to interpret and manage feelings productively.

Emotions are categorized, celebrated, repressed, adored, ignored, and medicated. Rarely, if ever, are they honored. Rarely, if ever, are they seen as energies. Emotions are not simply functions of brain chemistry. They are vital flowing forces that can help us communicate with others, if used effectively. I am a very emotional person. I can relate thoroughly with the problem of expressing emotions. Often in the work force you are expected to leave all your emotions at home and come prepared to do a task. How can one work without emotions?

Emotions play a role in how parties make sense of their relationships, degree of power, and social status. People constantly evaluate situations and events to feel out if they are personally relevant. These understandings and appraisals are infused with various emotions and feelings. Thus, emotion not only serves a side effect of conflict, but also frames the way in which parties understand and define their dispute.

Get inside your brain. Whenever mind images form in your mind, do you wonder something somewhere in your body? Most of the times you do. You are just unable to point out where exactly it is. Play around mentally and watch what you are doing inside. Your focal point is preoccupied. Your feeling will alter. Your brain can do so many wonderful things. You can also have fun creating various images and sounds by repeating something repeatedly in your head.

Watch your language. Your emotions are affected when you say something to yourself. Words may express your sensation. How you name it will affect your response. Keep away from careless language. Pick your words attentively when you talk to yourself. Avoid telling the things that you refuse to feel. Constant usage of negative words make you feel inadequate and defeated.

Embrace changes. When a calamity that causes grief engulf you, take action to overcome it. Don't allow your emotion of sadness to extend over a long period. Get busy. Always be sure of your actions at any given moment. Be very sure that your body and motions are under control all the time. Activities ignite your senses. Please treasure your happiness. You can improve state of mind through humor and laughter. Laughter is always the best medicine. Feelings and actions are interdependent. They can influence one another.

"You may not control all the events that happen to you, but you can decide not to be reduced by them."

~Maya Angelou

Sometimes you must eliminate to
elevate.

Sometimes you must give people a plate to go. Yes, feed them. But don't let allow them to sit at your table.

Surround yourself with people who
push you, who challenge you, who
make you laugh, who make you better,
and who make you happy.

You want to be comfortable, or you want to grow? 'Cause you can't do both.

Faith is seeing light with your heart,
when all your eyes see is darkness.

Emotional Balance Beam

I hate my emotions. I swear I do. The older I've gotten; I wish I could just throw certain emotions to the curb, like it was Sunday's news. I wish God would give me a Menu and let me choose the emotions I want LOL. Cause a lot of the ones he has given me, most days, I want to return to sender LOL! For most of my life I was able to control my emotions. I absolutely loved that about me. I thought it protected me. I thought it showcased my strength. The ability to feel miserable and all over the place internally. Externally, looking like one of the happiest and most put together people around...was always a blessing to me. It wasn't until I approached my mid-30s, that I realized it was also a curse.

It's like keeping a child sheltered. He or she will lack interpersonal skills. I, being sheltered/restricted from certain emotions, caused me to lack the necessary skills to cope and handle certain emotions when they arose. Anger and happiness I could handle and exhibit anytime with ease. Sadness, depression, despair, etc. – I would shut the hell down and become numb. Now my restriction on these emotions is weak and I hate it LOL! I HATE IT! I can't control or restrict these dang emotions at all. Although, in the moment I can't stand that loss of power. I noticed that there are added benefits. By the particular emotion being free to roam and do whatever, there are no side effects that linger and consume me. A result of this, is that it doesn't weigh me down as much – emotionally or mentally.

Avoidance doesn't work because pain is an inevitable part of life. It is an essential aspect of being human. It is in how we choose to respond to the emotional and physical pain we experience that determines whether we can get through that pain, or unwillingly extend and amplify it. Our wishful thinking tells us that if we can just avoid the pain, it won't affect us. Efforts to keep painful thoughts, feelings, and physical sensations at bay - may work temporarily. In the long run, it'll only prolong those experiences and intensify the suffering connected to them.

Developing emotional balance begins with a solid foundation of self-awareness, the heart of emotional intelligence. Self-Awareness enables us to recognize our emotions as they occur and the ways in which our emotions impact all aspects of our lives. Without Self-Awareness, we remain on autopilot and fall back on unquestioned behavioral responses and routines. To affect behavioral change; we must first become attuned to our emotions, and the ways in which they positively and negatively inform our lives.

According to Dan Mager, MSW, "Emotions, especially powerful and disturbing ones, can seem as though they will last forever. However, whether they are positive and bring smiles to our face and laughter to our lips, or painful and bring hurt to our hearts and tears to our eyes, feelings are always temporary. They come and go like guests who come to visit. Some are welcome and we're delighted to see them; others not so much."

Emotions of all types are felt within our mental consciousness, not within our senses. We certainly experience feelings within our senses, but the emotional reaction to whatever we engage with takes place always at the level of our mental consciousness within ourselves. From this perspective, emotions all have a degree of inaccuracy in the way they engage with the world. Rather than the actual object out there being what they engage with, it is a mental image of that object.

According to Psychology Today, "Being out of balance emotionally usually involves either not allowing yourself to experience your feelings as they evolve by avoiding or suppressing them, or being so attached to and identified with them that your feelings are all-consuming. Emotional balance occurs when we allow ourselves to feel whatever comes up, without feeling stifled or overwhelmed, and we learn to accept our feelings without judgment."

The Huffington Post, courtesy of Kino MacGregor (International Yoga Instructor & Author), provided nine easy tips for emotional balance. They are:

1. Breathing - Watch your breath throughout the day for signals about your stress level. If you notice yourself holding your breath, breathing erratically, or sighing often; consciously take 10 deep breaths, counting backwards with each inhalation and exhalation.

2. Practice Gratitude - Pause at regular integrals throughout the day and consciously find something that you are truly grateful for. Do

not act or pretend. In every stressful situation search for one thing that you can say an honest thanks about. Only the real attitude of gratitude has the power to change your emotional state.

3. Change Your Viewpoint - If you're stuck in the middle of intense emotions, you won't see clearly, and you will be reacting from past patterns. Act don't react. Consciously choose your actions from a place of clarity, rather than just reacting to pain or running toward pleasure. As soon as you notice yourself losing your emotional center, excuse yourself and change your view, literally!

4. Feel - So much tension and wasted energy is spent repressing or denying how we feel, both emotionally and in our bodies. Instead of pretending to be something that you are not, feel honestly what you are feeling and allow the simple truth of your emotions to set you

free. Every emotion surfaces to teach you something or tell you something. Your job is to be clear enough to recognize the emotion for the messenger that it is.

5. Use Your Senses - Direct your awareness to what you like about your current experience. Get fresh air and see the sunlight as much as possible. Notice and appreciate your surroundings.

6. Generate Energy - Little bursts of physical movement help the body feel better and the mind focus more intently. You don't have to run a marathon to be energized. Sometimes all it takes is a walk around the block or to go up and down a few flights of stairs. If you don't have time to get outside of your office, stand up in front of your desk for a few minutes every hour and either stretch or continue what you're doing while standing.

7. Reflect - Take the last moments of your day to reflect on the good things about your day. See the negative experiences as learning and evaluate from the perspective of what you can learn...not how you failed.

8. Dream - Let yourself daydream. Don't fill every moment of your day with Twitter, Facebook, and YouTube. Just let yourself relax and your mind wander. Be careful not to let your mind harp on the negative in these little reveries.

9. Surrender - Don't let yourself get too caught up in how things "should" be. Be prepared to let go of your attachments to any particular outcome so that you can be open to something bigger than you have ever imagined. Let life lead you down unexpected turns and you will discover magic in the most ordinary places.

"Care for your psyche…know thyself. For once we know ourselves, we may learn how to care for ourselves."

Me, Myself, And Faith

Everyone is on a road of difficulties and trials. We face these trials every day. Sometimes we work hard to resolve them. On the other hand, sometimes people will be afraid of the problems that come their way. We sometimes will try to escape it, but it will be there festering in our lives and in our minds. Until one day we decide to act; the time we decide to mend the problem is the day we can change and rid the problem from our lives for good. It is in the process of meeting and solving problems that life has its meaning. Problems are the cutting edge that distinguishes between success and failure. Problems call forth our courage and our wisdom. Indeed, they create our courage and our wisdom. It is only because of problems that we grow mentally and spiritually. When we desire to encourage the growth of the human spirit, we

challenge and encourage the human capacity to
solve problems.

Me and faith have been enemies most of my
life. We've reconciled! However, we tend to go up
and down like a seesaw. It is nowhere near where
I'd like our relationship to be. We are slightly in a
better place now, and one of my goals is to continue
working on it. My God it took a while to get there.
Prayer and therapy have truly taken me a long way.
Most of my life my faith has been faulty. Once I got
to my 30s, something shifted. I don't think it had
anything to do with the actual age of 30. I just
think that the year I turned 30, I just so happened
to look at things differently. God had me go through
somethings that taught me some lessons. Some
lessons I ignored, and some slapped me dead in my
face. Faith I always thought was an enemy. Faith
was something that for years I was afraid of and
confused about. For as long as I can remember my
grandma always beat me up over my head about

faith. Most times I wished she'd leave me alone but eventually what she would say to me sunk in and I got it......emphasis on eventually.

For me it was hard to have faith because as a child I felt as if things I love, I'd always lose. Things happened to me that I didn't understand. So, like most people I blamed God. How can I have faith in someone who has allowed me to experience such pain, confusion, stress, heartache, loss, and ailments? It was just hard for me to grasp faith. There would be moments when I had faith, but it was always shaky. Baby I could have faith and feel like it was as strong as Hercules. Let something happen and my faith just flows away in the wind like freshly permed hair on a windy day in Chicago.

Almost 40 years on this earth, I repeatedly screwed up and God still blessed me. I had a period where I took my eyes off him. He kept me. I got angry and he covered me. I stopped going to church. I wasn't consistent with my bible reading nor tithe paying. Yet, he still showed me favor. I sinned too many times and sometimes on purpose. Sometimes it was in desperation. God still called me. Times where it was felt that I was near death; times where I considered and attempted suicide, God's mercy still said no. Something happened as I looked back over my life. I should've been dead, in jail, or with a STD. Once again, mercy said no to all three.

I've been blessed and elevated. Opportunities fell into place. I realized there's an unconditional love that had been shown upon me. I wish I had improved my faith years ago. Especially in my early 20s. I learned from every mistake. Every test made me wiser and smarter. I wish it was easier. I wish God had tested me in easier ways. I may not agree with most of what God has done or allowed, but I understand. To whom much is given, much is required. Things must happen to test me in certain areas. Things must happen to me to ensure that I'm prepared for all the blessings that God has and will be bestowing upon me.

Faith is a day-by-day journey for me. It's not at all easy, but it is easier. I recognize certain things that must be in place internally, so that when things happen, I can adequately adapt. Many things I've learned as I look back over my life. One of the main things I've learned is that God never neglects the faithful. As I've continued to be faithful, as I've continued to use each day to be a better me, as I've continued to use each day to get closer to God....no matter, God has allowed me to land on my feet. Heck in some situations he's allowed me to turn out better than I was before the situation occurred.

Turning intellectual faith into our personal possession is always a fight, not just sometimes. God brings us into circumstances to educate our faith, because the nature of faith is to make the object of our faith very real to us. Until we know

134

Jesus, God is merely a concept, and we can't have faith in Him. Faith always works in a personal way because the purpose of God is to see that perfect faith is made real in His children. Oswald Chambers once said: "Common sense and faith are as different from each other as natural life is from the spiritual, and as impulsiveness is from inspiration. Nothing that Jesus Christ ever said is common sense, but is revelation sense, and is complete...whereas common sense falls short. Yet, faith must be tested and tried before it becomes real in your life."

The term "faith" has numerous connotations and is used in different ways, often depending on context. James W. Fowler (1940-2015) proposes a series of stages of faith-development (or spiritual development) across the human lifespan. His stages relate closely to the work of Piaget, Erikson, and Kohlberg regarding aspects of psychological development in children and adults. Fowler defines faith as an activity of trusting, committing, and relating to the world based on a set of assumptions of how one is related to others and the world. Fowler's Stages of Faith are:

1. Intuitive-Projective: a stage of confusion and of high impressionability through stories and rituals. (Pre-school period)
2. Mythic-Literal: a stage where provided information is accepted in order to conform to social norms. (School-going period)
3. Synthetic-Conventional: In this stage the faith acquired is concreted in the belief system with the forgoing of personification and replacement with authority in individuals or groups that represent one's beliefs. (early-late adolescence)
4. Individuative-Reflective: In this stage, the individual critically analyzes adopted and accepted faith with existing systems of faith. Disillusion or strengthening of faith happens

in this stage. Based on needs, experiences, and paradoxes. (Early adulthood)

5. Conjunctive faith: In this stage people realize the limits of logic and facing the paradoxes or transcendence of life, accept the "mystery of life" and often return to the sacred stories and symbols of the pre-acquired or re-adopted faith system. This stage is called negotiated settling in life. (Mid-life)

6. Universalizing faith: This is the "enlightenment" stage where the individual comes out of all the existing systems of faith and lives life with universal principles of compassion and love and in service to others for upliftment, without worries and doubt. (Middle - late adulthood (45-65 yrs and plus)

Regardless of which approach to faith a Christian take, all agree that the Christian faith is aligned with the ideals and the example of the life of

Jesus. The Christian sees the mystery of God and his grace. They seek to know and become obedient to God. To a Christian, faith is not static but causes one to learn more of God and to grow. Christian faith has its origin in God. Faith is not only fideism or simple obedience to a set of rules or statements. Before Christians have faith, they must understand in whom and in what they have faith. Without understanding there cannot be true faith. That understanding is built on the foundation of the community of believers, the scriptures and traditions, and on the personal experiences of the believer. British Christian apologist John Lennox argues that "faith conceived as belief that lacks warrant, is very different from faith conceived as belief that has warrant". He states that "the use of the adjective 'blind' to describe 'faith' indicates that faith is not necessarily, always, or indeed normally - blind". "The validity, or warrant, of faith or belief depends on the strength of the evidence on which the belief is based."

Faith is the only power that inspires a human being in despair. But if a person loses faith during the period of struggle, he gives up hope for any success and succumbs to the unfavorable situations. So, an individual without faith is as good as a dead person. His life is just like a deflated balloon. So, we can truly conclude that faith is the foundation stone of any project that is undertaken with a will to complete. It is that driving force which enlightens the candle of hope by giving strength to fight against all odds. A person having faith may face failures in his or her life, but he does not lose his heart in despair.

A person can set a goal for himself, only if he has faith that ultimately, he will achieve the goal. Faith forms the foundation of every new achievement, every invention, every discovery, and every new victory. There is a co-relation between faith and achievement. Faith is not about belief. Faith in fact has very little to do with what beliefs you hold, other than that it allows you to hold them. Faith is a sacred, deep, and emotionally involved kind of trust. Faith is the kind of trust that you enter with your whole being. Faith is the kind of trust that, when it has been broken, it hurts deep inside. Faith is the kind of trust that finds a way to trust again despite the hurt.

> "Faith consists of believing when it is beyond the power of reason to believe."
>
> ~Voltaire

I am better than I used to be. Better
than I was yesterday. But hopefully
not as good as I'll be tomorrow.

Switch your mentality from "I'm broken and helpless" to "I'm growing and healing" and watch how your life changes, for the better.

Don't let your loyalty become slavery.
If they don't appreciate what you bring
to the table, let them eat alone.

Feeling down, lost, confused, angry, jealous are all parts of the human condition. Don't fight them…accept them…love them and go beyond them.

~Maxine Lagace

Your past is a lesson...not a life
sentence. Forgive yourself and focus
on the future.

-Mel Robbins

Nothing is more beautiful than the smile that has struggled through the tears.

-Demi Lovato

You Done Made It Through

Pause...look at yourself...think...exhale! Let's re-examine. Let's try and look at it from a different perspective. The white flag is looking attractive right now and/or it has many times before. You get closer and closer. Drugs, weapons, vehicle, jail, homeless, demotivated are all diverse vessels able and willing to get you closer to that white flag. Something got in the way. You don't feel like it was anything you did. Is a past prayer being answered? Is it finally your turn for a miracle? Before you knew it...you exhaled – looked around...you done made it through!

Trauma has piled up! You've lost a lot of people and things that you've loved. You don't trust. The negative experiences swarm about you like a beehive – you're trapped. Hungry, hopeless, lonely, broke...entranced by trauma. Joy is forgotten and taboo. You no longer recognize the person in the mirror. Guilt and re-infected wounds have you at the edge of the cliff with dangling feet. Something shifted! So numb and detached from life, you missed it. You don't feel like it was anything you did. Ancestor's prayers? Maybe. Unexpected good Samaritan or karma paying you some of what you're owed? Possibly. Before you knew it...you exhaled – looked around...you done made it through!

God has pissed you off. Resentment with him, you, and life just exudes from every fiber of your being. You dread waking up. You dread sleeping. A life that has left you broken, battered, and shattered awaits you. When will it end? When will wounds start to heal and pieces slowly reconnect? When will your heart smile again? You walk around anxious and agitated, waiting for the next negative thing that is going to happen to you. That's become your new normal. That's become the most consistent thing in your life, occurring weekly, like the release of your favorite show's new episode. Something is different. Like a week off during NFL season, is this your bye week? Has the hem of his garment been touched? Has light illuminated your dark places? Before you knew it...you exhaled – looked around...you done made it through!

He, she, they disappointed you...betrayed you and hurt you. You were loyal when it wasn't deserved. You covered for 'em when they didn't deserve it. You upheld, turned the other cheek, loved without conditions, revolved your life around them, put them first, and many chances were given – unappreciated. You did all this knowingly and willingly, knowing the whole while ties needed to be severed. Heartbroken more, trust extensively damaged, self-worth tainted, self-validation lost, and the whole while hiding it all inside. Embarrassed? Mad at yourself? Both? Transition and evolution are busy and has taken you on a ride. You remember pride and joy. You remember confidence. You've been re-introduced to you! You were defeated! Passion and joy ceased. You don't know how or when it occurred. Was it support from an unexpected friend? Was it the essence of your foundation re-connecting? Was it your journey back to basics? Because...look...one day soon this will be one of my testimonies... before you knew it...you exhaled – looked around...you done made it through!

"A bend in the road is not the end of the road...unless you fail to make the turn."

~Helen Keller

Stay private!
Stay low-key!
Stay humble!

There are rare people who will show up
at the right time, help you through the
hard times, and stay into your best
times...those are the keepers.

~Nausicaa Twila

When you know who you are, you
aren't phased by the misconceptions of
others. Know thyself…love thyself.

Protection Of Peace

Protecting your peace. I didn't know what that meant. I didn't care. I had no idea the benefits that it would have for me emotionally, mentally, physically, and spiritually. There is no blueprint for one protecting their peace. It will vary by individual. However, there is one common denominator. There is one common priority.

I thought I was some kind of superman. It was as if all that I had to give, internally, was an unlimited supply. One of my main issues was feeling like my validation and happiness was connected to the amount of people in my life or what they needed from me. I blindly felt like my validation and happiness depended on what one's opinion of me was. I was willing to sacrifice joy and peace, for what I needed. I wasn't realizing that I was feeding, not what I needed but what was harming me...not what I needed – but what the wrong aspects of my ego wanted.

For me, protecting my peace looks like:

1. If it doesn't put a smile on my face, I'm not doing it or I'm not going.

2. If I don't have it in me to give, I can't pour it into someone else. I mess around and am depleted, and don't have anything to take care of myself. Most people won't care about me being depleted, if I am being what they need me to be for them.

3. Saying no with no explanation.

4. Removing people out of my life or distancing myself from people that add nothing positive to my life. Their presence did nothing for my life. Therefore, their absence won't mean a

thing. Also, doing this with no explanation.

5. Feeding myself spiritually daily...no matter what.

6. If entertaining certain energies, foolishness, and/or individuals isn't going to serve me a purpose – exit stage left and pay them dust.

On top of all the unwanted emotions you may go through when dealing with someone toxic, don't forget that your body is feeling them as well. Those negative feelings and frustrations cause immediate stress on the body. If you are constantly worrying and angry, your body is already on its own journey of increased heart rate, high blood pressure, anxiety, and panic attacks.

No one is exempt from the aforementioned list. History, family ties, organizational affiliations, friendships, or positive memories won't make anyone the exception. To have sustainability with this, it is my responsibility to ensure I'm consistently sticking to this. Otherwise, I'm doing a disservice to myself. Otherwise, I'm getting in my way and God's way.

Some people are peace stealers. They always have problems, always need your help, and are always in crisis mode. They expect you to come running, to cheer them up, to keep them encouraged. And if you don't, they make you feel guilty. You love them, but they continually dump their problems on you. Often, we encounter these energy draining sources that leave us feeling depleted, but we hesitate to directly confront the situation. If we don't think about it too much, it couldn't possibly hurt us. Right?

Love yourself enough to treat yourself. You don't deserve to feel less than. You don't have to measure up to the expectations others place on you. Love yourself enough to have standards. Sometimes, you are going to have to be the bittersweet lesson for those who do not know how to treat their blessings. Protecting your peace is crucial to living a purpose filled and empowered life. Remember to protect your peace like your life depends on it... 'cause it does.

Good humans don't make you feel like you don't matter. Here's the thing, we all have lives. We have jobs, families, and goals etc. It's hard to find time for things, but we do. We find time for things that matter to us (read that sentence again). If you find yourself in a place where you simply feel unwanted because a person isn't treating you the way you deserve to be treated, then note it, accept it, and move forward.

Next time you come across a not so welcoming feeling in your gut, next time you feel drained trying to explain to someone how you feel, and next time you are upset because of something another person has done recklessly...protect your peace.

Between what works for me and doing some research, I came across a list of ways that could possibly be very beneficial to aid you in protecting your peace.

    a. Say no
    b. Practice listening to your intuition
    c. Cut the ties
    d. Nourish your body
    e. Be conscious of your thoughts
    f. De-clutter
    g. Social Media cleanse
    h. Release toxic energies
    i. Find a quiet space
    j. Focus on what's important

"Peace brings with it so many positive emotions that it is worth aiming for in all circumstances."

~Estella Eliot

From A Mind In Pieces 2 A Peace of Mind

Peace of mind is something we all seem to want and want more of. A few of us get it. When we do, it tends to be fleeting. I think the reason has something to do with how we think of peace of mind. It is not something we can have and hold, but it is certainly something that we can learn to cultivate and allow to grow.

Having peace of mind can be one of the most freeing states of being. It takes work to acquire it and to sustain it. Many times, we allow people, places, and things to get in the way of us achieving peace within. Until one acknowledges, appreciates, and respects themselves; peace of mind will be hard to acquire or easy to acquire, but hard to keep. I truly feel that when one has peace of mind, it equips them to easily handle and combat stress, or any negative situation. Peace of mind is a state of mental and emotional calmness. It comes with no worries, fears, or stress. The mind is quiet, and you experience a sense of happiness and freedom.

When you think of the times you have experienced real peace of mind, have there not been times when outwardly there were problems? Peace manifests when the incessant inner chatter of the mind slows down. When it appears; anxiety, stress, worries, fear, mental and emotional restlessness, nervousness, and impatience disappear. It is a state of inner calmness, tranquility, and serenity. It brings forth happiness, tolerance, inner poise, inner balance, and self-control. Peace of mind is an acquired skill that requires time, practice, and perseverance to develop. It is just like any other skill. With the right training, desire, motivation, patience, and perseverance - you are sure to attain at least some degree of inner peace.

You don't have to wait for the perfect circumstances to start working on gaining it. Regardless of the life you're living, or irrespective of your circumstances, you can start here and now. This might require some effort on your part. However, it is a worthwhile project, and the rewards are great. The restless mind jumps from one thought to another. It allows thoughts to come and go incessantly from morning till night, giving us no rest for a moment. Most of these thoughts are not exactly invited. They just come, occupy our attention for a while, and then disappear - making room for others.

Thoughts are like clouds drifting through the sky. Like the clouds, they are not permanent. Due to their incessant movement, they distract our attention and disturb our focus. This activity of the restless mind occupies our attention all the time. Now our attention is on this thought, and then on another one. We spend a lot of energy and attention on these passing thoughts. With most of them being unimportant, wasting our time and energy.

When you do not have peace of mind, you aid yourself in being vulnerable to high levels of stress. I think that minimal levels of stress are important and can be essential. You can utilize various tools you've learned, as far as stress management; you can see just how strong you are, you can see who is really in your corner, and many more. However, high levels of stress aren't good for anyone. Stress can kill you. Many ailments and illnesses can be acquired or worsened by levels of stress.

A state of peace of mind leads to better emotional and physical health, increased energy, stronger mental powers, improved memory, and a better ability to learn and study. It also helps you handle your daily affairs of life in a more efficient manner. It eases stress and enables you to act calmly in a poised manner, in difficult situations. We live in a world where worries, strain and restlessness abound. You might think that there is nothing to do about it, and therefore, accept this situation as an inevitable evil, but you don't have to. You can experience inner peace even under stressful conditions and circumstances, but it does not come instantly. It is developed gradually and through training.

In my life, I've had sporadic and quick bouts of having a peace of mind. It was always so difficult for me to have a peace of mind because I would:

1. Trust the wrong people
2. Be in desperate situations and make the wrong decisions
3. Give people too many chances after they've already showed me who they are
4. Strayed away from my basics
5. Lose focus
6. Be too guarded and hold too much inside. Thus, not allowing myself to heal or release

It wasn't until the end of my early 30s, when I finally experienced what it was like to have peace of mind for an extended amount of time. That doesn't mean I didn't or don't have trials, tribulations, highly stressful moments, or negative moments. I still have all of those occurring, but not as often. I can handle situations so much better. I can live a freer life. I'm more conscious about taking care of myself internally and externally, no matter what.

Lord knows it took a long time for me to get to this point. I had a lot to deal with, to acknowledge, to release myself from, and to admit. After so many years of not having a peace of mind, of not being happy, of being so broken and numb internally...how was I able to get to the point that I'm at now? In short, the things I had to do...and in no order, were:

1. No matter how uncomfortable something was I had to talk about it

2. I had to acknowledge and be accountable with anything I did wrong to myself or others

3. Realize the ones who I needed to keep at a distance or completely remove them from my life

4. Find out what makes me happy and keep that #1 in my life no matter what

5. Just like I must feed myself physically every day...I needed to feed myself spiritually everyday

6. Stop seeking validation in other's needs or opinions of me

7. Saying no and not feeling guilty

8. Understanding that some people come into my life for a time and a season. There may be certain people that I want, or thought would be in my life forever. I must accept that for some, the season is over, and I need to let them go or let the chips fall where they may

9. Go to therapy

In doing research on this topic, I came across 2 websites. The 2 websites are Psychology Today and Success Consciousness. With information I learned from both websites, here are some tips in acquiring and sustaining a peace of mind:

- Allow yourself time to just sit without distractions, without something to do, or a place to go. No multitasking.
- Use that time for you and get curious about your mind and experience, just as it is. Look into your experience and just watch the goings on between your ears and in your heart. There is nothing to do and no state to achieve. Just practice being exactly where you are just as you are.
- You can breathe into each moment and imagine leaning into it with a sense of curiosity and with a kind intention to

just watch and be at peace. As you do that, you can watch and let go with each in breath and out breath.

- Notice the urge to change the experience or to pull out. These are the red flags that your old history is showing up with all the old habits that's compelling you to change your mind and body. In short, to be something other than you are. These habits are the fuel for struggle, and if you practice just noticing them as thoughts and urges, reminders of the past --"ah, there's my old history, or there's a thought that..." -- you interrupt the old programming and disarm it.
- Stay away from negative conversations and from negative people. You don't want their thoughts and words to sink

into your subconscious mind and affect your mood and state of mind.

- Stay away from negative conversations and from negative people. You don't want their thoughts and words to sink into your subconscious mind and affect your mood and state of mind.

- Accept what cannot be changed. This saves a lot of time, energy, and worries. Consistently, we face numerous inconveniences, irritations, and situations that are beyond our control. If we can change them, that's fine, but this is not always possible. We must learn to put up with such things and accept them cheerfully.

"Nobody can bring you peace but yourself."

~Ralph Waldo Emerson

PEACE: Gift, Treasure, And Power

Peace of mind and relaxation is so freakin' important to me. I can't even explain how important it is in my daily life. In my 20s, it wasn't a priority nor was I aware of its importance. As a teen or younger, I didn't even know or care about peace of mind or relaxing. I was just constantly on the go, constantly searching for something, constantly running from something, and constantly being of service or use to others. This in some ways caused me to go through life with it being a blur and numbness.

Be it that I am hugely ambitious and hardworking, it is important for me to understand the need for rejuvenation. I don't like just one income, nor do I like just having one thing going on in my life. Listen....even times where my health wasn't what it should've been, I was still working towards some kind of goal that had nothing to do with my current situation at that time. I spent a lot of my life making others a priority. Going places because they wanted me to go, doing things because they wanted me to do it, putting on this persona or identity...or at least trying to...because it was who certain people wanted me to be.

I would ignore what I wanted and needed, because it was as if my validation and happiness lied in being used for other's purpose. Their opinion and feelings, I allowed to dictate my life. This caused me to allow or ignore things in certain friendships/relationships that I normally wouldn't. It caused me to be loyal to people who didn't deserve it. It caused me to give so much of myself and never getting anything back in return. It was like a bank account. You spend all your money and when there's nothing coming back your account is in the negative, unless you don't have no overdraft protection on your account (LOL). That's how I was emotionally, mentally, and spiritually. I gave of myself completely to others and their drama or situation. When I would go through my stuff, I ignored it or neglected it. I continued to give give give. I wasn't getting anything back. This caused me on MANY occasions to be emotionally, mentally, and spiritually broken...numb...exhausted.

I realized what made me happy. I realized the harm I had been doing to myself all these 25+ years, by neglecting myself. I realized the relationships and friendships that had to go. I realized the necessary tools and facets in my life that I needed to acquire or improve, if I wanted to be the best me I could be, and reach the potential that God was and is orchestrating for me. I've never been so happy in my life. Shoulders back, head high, love and peace in my heart, clear sight for discernment, and a necessary people purge. This has aided in solidifying my renewed foundation and sense of being. People purge was one of the top 3 components that helped me to get where I am. Anyone who is not conducive to the life I work hard for, the person I am and am still becoming, the standards I have for myself and my life...they got to go. I don't care if we share bloodline, organizational affiliations, life experiences, or sexual fluids.

One of the many things I've realized recently is that I can maneuver through life's hurdles. I am strong. I deserve happiness. I can accept nothing less than my worth, with no exceptions. The requirements that I have for people who are to be in my life romantically, platonically, professionally, and with my family; if the expectations and requirements aren't met, they are either distanced or thrown out of my life faster than Usain Bolt can run 100 meters.

You know too much stress is not good for you, but you can't help it. There's never enough time. It appears that certain levels of stress never go away. So, you accept stress as it is. You stay stressed thinking it's your fate. There are people who need to handle even bigger responsibilities, goals, busier schedules, and more relationships. Most of them burn out. Some refuse to stay stressed. The difference between the stressed and the calm is not the amount of load in life. It's how they handle the load.

It's easy to relax when life is all good and you have the time. Relaxing is the act of consciously taking time for yourself to recharge and lower your stress hormone level. It could mean a good night's sleep, a walk in nature, a long meditation session, taking a shower, watching Netflix, or whichever way you wish to relax. Relaxation is the cure for stress. Keeping calm is the prevention. It is the skill of having peace of mind despite the chaos of life. It requires you to not let the environment affect your cortisol level.

Chronic stress harms the pre-frontal cortex of your brain which regulates memory, attention, behavior, emotions, and thoughts. This also includes decision making and planning. All these are critical for high-performance. When your cortisol levels stay high, you live in survival mode. Your amygdala region of the brain stays activated which is responsible for the fight-or-flight response. When you stay calm, you keep your cortisol under control and use your pre-frontal cortex to live proactively.

A peaceful place is somewhere you can go to slow down, reflect, and engage in enjoyable activities. You can be alone or with others who you find relaxing to be around. A place that doesn't demand anything of you or expects you to be someone you're not. A place where you can just be. In your own space, you can be noisy or quiet. You can work on activities and interests that you are passionate about. You can read or otherwise escape life's daily stresses and routines. Other options besides a special room in the home include the bathtub, backyard or community garden, and a nearby park.

When you're at peace; when you are engaged with life while also feeling relatively relaxed, calm, and safe – you are protected from stress. Your immune system grows stronger, and you become more resilient. Your outlook brightens and you see more opportunities. In relationships, feeling at peace prevents overreactions. It increases the odds of being treated well by others and supports you in being clear and direct when you need to be.

Having the peace that passeth all understanding is a powerful tool for anyone to have in their life. It makes room for rejuvenation, reflection, health, and destiny. It aids in bringing us to our center...to our nucleus...any kind of damage control or adapting is easier, and our entire internal infrastructure is sustainable.

A website entitled, Exploring Your Mind, provided 7 steps to having relaxation and peace of mind:

1. Set limits
2. Find a relaxation technique that works for you
3. Do not make a mountain of a molehill
4. Slow down
5. Put your world in order and throw out what you have too much of or don't need (people or things)
6. Accept and let go
7. Solve your problems now

"You should feel beautiful, and you should feel safe. What you surround yourself with should bring you peace of mind and peace of spirit."

~Stacy London

Love and peace of mind do protect us.
They allow us to overcome the
problems that life hands us. They
teach us to survive... to live now... to
have the courage to confront each day.

~Bernie Siegel

You'll never find peace of mind until you listen to your heart.

~George Michael

Peace is the result of retraining your mind to process life as it is, rather than as you think it should be.

~Wayne W. Dyer

If there's no inner peace, people can't give it to you. Your husband can't give it to you. Your children can't give it to you. You must give it to you.

~Linda Evans

Peace is a day-to-day problem, the product of a multitude of events and judgments. Peace is not an "is", it is a "becoming".

~Haile Selassie

Mirror Mirror: The Power of Self-Awareness

Self-Awareness for me is and was powerful. It took a lot of falling, breakthroughs, and obstacles for me to conduct a personal self-awareness analysis. I had to take it seriously. I had to do the hard work and make the proper modifications. When self-awareness became concrete, self-love improved. Peace of mind and other internal aspects, such as confidence and joy, could be sustained. When concrete self-awareness is joined by joy, confidence, and happiness about yourself; there's a foundation and way of being that is indestructible. When hate and negativity try to visit, you won't falter or be broken.

Self-development starts at a very young age. When a preschooler is asked how they are different from other children, they usually look at their self-concept. Self-Concept is their identity of their set of beliefs about what they are like as individuals. Most preschoolers give inaccurate statements about their self-concept. They usually overestimate their skills and knowledge. Preschool-Age children also begin to develop a view of self that reflects their culture. Children's views of self become more differentiated. As they get older, children discover that they may be good at some things and not so good at others.

Children's self-concepts become divided into personal and academic spheres. During middle childhood children begin social comparison. Social comparison is the desire to evaluate one's own behavior, abilities, expertise, and opinions by comparing them to those of others. During middle childhood, children deal with the crisis industry versus inferiority stage. The stage is characterized by a focus on efforts to attain competence in meeting the challenges presented by parents, peers, school, and other complexities of the modern world.

This is a time of their life where the child develops self-esteem. Self-Esteem is an individual's overall positive and negative self-evaluation. Self-Concept reflects beliefs and cognitions about the self. Self-esteem is more emotionally oriented.

Everyone is aware, that's no big deal. Awareness can be developed as a skill set, just as talking can be developed by learning a broader vocabulary. The more you know different kinds of things to pay attention to, the more you can choose (or not) to use that information. Self-Awareness is the first component of emotional intelligence. This means knowing one's internal states, preferences, resources, and intuition. This goes up to the level of being, who am I, what are my resources, what do I prefer, and what makes me happy. Individuals who have these traits are not acute, but rather have interest in themselves and the people around them. In order words, self-awareness in an individual can be identified by his or her self-confidence. Where one will not feel threatened by change, but rather could embrace change and see all change as being positive.

We might quickly assume that we are self-aware, but it is helpful to have a relative scale for awareness. If you have ever been in an auto accident, you may have experienced everything happening in slow motion and noticed details of your thought process and the event. This is a state of heightened awareness. With practice, we can learn to engage these types of heightened states and see new opportunities for interpretations in our thoughts, emotions, and conversations. Having awareness creates the opportunity to make changes in behavior and beliefs. Self-Awareness is developed through practices in focusing your attention on the details of your personality and behavior. It isn't learned from reading a book. When you read a book, you are focusing your attention on the conceptual ideas in the book. You can develop an intellectual understanding of the ideas of self-awareness from a book, but this is not the same. With your attention in a book, you are practicing not paying attention to your own behavior. As well as your emotions and personality.

It is quite difficult in today's time to find time to think about who we are. As well as what our strengths, weaknesses, personalities, habits, and values are. Besides, many of us are not just inclined to spend much time on self-reflection. Many of us have a low level of self-awareness because self-awareness is an essential first step toward maximizing management skills. It can improve our judgment. It can help us identify opportunities for professional development and personal growth.

Self-Awareness helps us explore our strengths and cope without weaknesses. If we are good at "seeing the big picture" that surrounds decisions, but not as good at focusing on the details; we might want to consult colleagues and subordinates that are more detail oriented when making major decisions. Cooperation between big-picture-oriented decision makers and detail-oriented decision makers can produce high quality decisions.

Self-Awareness is empowering because it can reveal where the performance problems are and indicate what can be done to improve performance. In addition, awareness of your psychological needs can increase your motivation by helping you understand and seek out the rewards that you really desire such as a sense of accomplishment, additional responsibility, an opportunity to help others, or a flexible work schedule. Always keep on motivating yourself, that is the best way for motivation.

It is important for every individual to understand themselves. If you can understand yourself, you will understand others easily.

Communication with others will be easier for you. Different self-awareness questions, methods, and studies can help us discover things about ourselves that we did not know. We can find out about our hidden and unknown sides. Being open to feedback from others can make us stronger.

Developing self-awareness can help us to identify when we are stressed out or under pressure. It is also often a must for real communication and interpersonal relations, as well as for developing empathy for others. Self-Awareness is the ability to choose feelings being felt, rather than just thinking the thoughts that are encouraged from the increasing events leading up to the situations of the moment. Self-Awareness is important because if you want to change your life in any way, you need to know yourself before you can act. You need to know what you need to do to head in the right direction and you can't do that until you know yourself.

Setting goals not only gives a road map for success, but it shows you the best alternatives you should need or desire a change along the way. We should review our goals on a regular basis. Many do this daily as it helps them assess their progress and gives them the ability to make faster more informed decisions. Having a clear understanding of your thought and behavior patterns helps you understand other people. This ability to empathize facilitates better personal and professional relationships.

"Self-Awareness is the ability to take an honest look at your life without any attachments to it being right or wrong, good or bad."

~Debbie Ford

Save the excuses. It's not about having time. It's about making time. If it matters, you will make time.

Make yourself unavailable for negative
situations and conversations and
watch how quickly the positive ones
take their place.

Through every walk of pain, there is
always a step of happiness that
awaits.

Don't speak negatively about yourself,
even as a joke. Your body doesn't
know the difference. Words are energy
and cast spells that's why it's called
spelling. Change the way you speak
about yourself, and you can change
your life. What you're not changing,
you're also choosing.

~Bruce Lee

Growth happens by doing things you
are unqualified to do.

Believe in yourself and you will be
unstoppable.

Focus on your breakthrough, not
those who tried to break you.

~Carlos King

If you prioritize yourself, you are going
to save yourself.

~Gabrielle Union

Opportunity is missed by most people
because it is dressed in overalls and
looks like work.

~Thomas Edison

You define your own life. Don't let
other people write your script.

~Oprah Winfrey

It is our choices that show what we really are, far more than our abilities.

~J.K. Rowling

If plan "A" didn't work, the alphabet
has 25 letters. Stay cool.

Don't let any failure take up too much
of your time. Standup, regroup and get
right back in the game.

You've outgrown the version of you that needed to survive. It's time to become the version of you that's here to thrive.

It Takes A Village

Having a village is essential to a person thriving and surviving. A village, which can also be referred to as a support system, can provide an individual with practical and emotional support. As life evolves and changes, it is expected that the village will be modified. An individual's village can be affected negatively or positively, by a variety of factors. These factors could be a change of standards, modified expectations, trauma, consistency, heartbreak, and more. As individuals mature and start to have various life experiences; their village could expand a little bit, because of an increase in socializing or various avenues that could have them interact with a plethora of more people.

Growing up, I knew the phrase, "It takes a village to raise a child". However, I felt that all I needed was my grandparents. My grandparents were my parents. Due to the deep bond, we shared, I didn't feel like I needed anyone but them. What I thought I needed, wasn't what God gave me. I was blessed with having some amazing relationships with neighbors, individuals that were friends of my grandparents, and fellow church members. Blood couldn't make us any thicker or tighter. Many have been like family to me, more so than most of the ones I'm related to. Without their support, guidance, tough love, lectures, and good times; I can't imagine what my childhood would've been like.

The older I got the more I realized three impactful things about having a village. The first one is, my village was brought together by default. I had no control as to the people I was around because I was a child. Much of my village was going to be individuals that my parental unit brought around me. As I got older, my village was modified because I became an adult. As an adult, I have control as to who is or isn't in my life. Individuals were moved around or completely removed, based on a variety of reasons. These reasons are emotional and mental health, social life, my priorities, authenticity, trauma, various commonalities, mutual give and take, various habits (good, bad, indifferent), and no yes men (or women). I didn't feel that I had gotten it right, as far as those who were a part of my village, until my 30s. Two important major keys, in the words of DJ Khaled, had to be present. Those are consistent and they had to be a safe place for me. The same level of reproach that I hold people at is the same level of reproach that I make sure I'm at. We must trust one another. We must be each other's safe place. Whether it be a situation that's good, bad, or indifferent. The relationship must also be a mutual give and take, not a one-sided one.

Support systems are critical for anyone to have. Many people think that it is easier to do things alone and that their own health is something only they should be worrying about. This is not the case at all. While it is important to do some things on your own, having a support system that is there for you when things get tough is critical to maintaining your mental and physical health. To really make strides in improving yourself or building new skills, you must ensure you have the right people surrounding you. Having a good support system is the key to a healthy and balanced life. This support will be the one that you can open up to when you need to talk, and be a listener when others need to talk to you. Social support and interactions are the backbone of living a well-rounded life but can be challenging to find at times.   Support systems are often identified as 3 main groups. These groups are family, friends, and work colleagues (either a friend or mentor). The type of support received by each group will usually look quite different. Emotional support is usually received from friends and family. Emotional support is inclusive of empathy, love, and trust. This group will usually be the one you turn to when you need to get something off your chest or a shoulder to lean on. These are the people you can rely on to help keep your mental health sane. This group can also offer tangible support. An example of this being you get stuck in a meeting and can't take your child to their appointment, so your mother picks them up and takes them. Work colleagues and mentors offer support on a more professional and career level. They can help you if you're struggling with any issues at work or help you plan out the next step in your career. Work plays a big part of everyday life. So having these strong support systems in place can significantly improve your mood and overall mindset.

Vantage Point Recovery, a treatment center for various mental health conditions, states that there are 5 traits that need to be present to ensure

that you have a healthy mentality and lifestyle.
Those traits are:

1. Accountability
2. Fellowship
3. Education
4. Psychosocial Services (e.g. pastor, therapist, life coach, etc.)
5. Purpose

Your village is set in place, not so that you can have "yes men" surrounding you all the time. You do not need to build a clique or posse. You are creating a group of people where you all offer each other inspiring assistance, tough love at times, and the fulfillment of joy on this journey called life. Every single person deserves to have a village that does this. If your village doesn't do this for you, then you're not moving through life with a village...you're moving through life with captivity.

Dr. Debra O'Shea, an anxiety specialist, states that there are 5 advantages of having a strong village/support system. They are:

1. Sense of belonging: A sense of belonging is important throughout our lives. We need to thrive, not just survive.

2. Reduce Stress: A strong village aids in stress reduction. Venting and spending time with loved ones can help reduce our anxiety and increase our mood.

3. Improve overall health and wellbeing: A good village helps with our overall physical health throughout our lives and especially as we age.

4. Emotional support: A strong village is pertinent to good emotional health as it gives us a community of support during trying times.

5. Improved self-esteem: When we have people we can rely on and who can rely on us for support, we feel better about ourselves. It is

always good to feel as though we have some people rooting for us on the sidelines as well as rooting for those in our village.

Decide on the individuals that you believe will have a positive influence, which will improve your life. You can make a list of the individuals you know who are already in your corner. This can include anyone from family and friends to counselors and people in the community. Then choose those who respect you, who you trust, who make you feel safe and comfortable, who you feel happier and more positive with, and those who bring out the best in you.

"I'm lucky to have a great support system in my friends and some of my family. If you have those people that you trust, go ahead, fall back into them, and let them be your hammock and cocoon...let them embrace you."

~Joanna Noelle Levesque

Live without pretending.
Love without depending.
Listen without defending.
Speak without offending.

~Drake

You carry so much love in your heart.
Give some to yourself.

An arrow can only be shot by pulling it backward. So, when life is dragging you back with difficulties, it means that it's going to launch you into something great. So just focus and keep aiming.

~Paulo Coelho

You don't need to find yourself. You're
not lost. You need to remember who
you were before the world got to you.
That's where your power lies.

Self-love, self-respect, self-worth...there is a reason they all start with "self". You cannot find them in anyone else.

One of the most important days is the day you decide you're good enough for you. It's the day you set yourself free.

~Brittany Josephina

Mirror mirror
On the wall,
I'll always get up
After I fall.
And whether I run,
Walk, or have to crawl
I'll set my goals
And achieve them all.

Attention:
Stop giving people do-overs who treat
you like
leftovers!

Believe in yourself and all that you are. Know that there is something inside you that is greater than any obstacle.

-Christian D. Larson

If it doesn't bring peace, profits, or
purpose...then don't give it your time,
energy, or attention.

Discipline + Focus + Action = Success

Just when you open your eyes first thing in the morning, take a deep breath and say: "Today, I am going to be better". Trust me, it will do you wonders.

Don't wish for it
Work for it

Life becomes easier when you learn to
accept the apology you never got.

Stop trying to invite God into a relationship HE told you to stay out of.

Everywhere I go I prosper. Everything I do always works out for me. I welcome new energy. I am attracting better. I feel good about who I am. I love myself. I choose to be hopeful. I believe in myself. I am thriving in every way. Things are happening for me now.

~Idil Ahmed

Learn to love the sound of your feet
walking away from things not meant
for you.

You can't heal in the same
environment that made you sick.

What's meant for you will always feel natural, calm, and clear – not forced, chaotic, and confused.

It is not hard to acquire the right village…the right tribe. You just have to make space. You must remove some people from your life or remove yourself out of other's life. You must make space and you do not have to announce your departure. You do not owe them an explanation nor a reason why.

~Jill Scott

Don't let fear hold you back: fear of what people are going to think. If they're not for you, then you don't need them. Your destiny is not dependent on everyone being for you.

Dear Lord,

Today push me out of my slump, help me get over what almost took me under, get me out my feelings and into my faith, and pull out of me all the gifts you put in me.

Worrying does not take away
tomorrow's troubles. It takes away
today's peace.

There will be obstacles. There will be doubters. There will be mistakes. But with hard work, there are no limits.

~Michael Phelps

Start where you are. Use what you
have. Do what you can.

~Arthur Ashe

Living With A Purpose

There are multiple ways in which one could have a purpose filled life. There are times in which this can vary. This can be affected by one's growth, maturity (or lack thereof), self-esteem, motivation, and many other factors. For most of my life, I thought being of service gave my life purpose. I would constantly make myself accessible. I would constantly put others' wants and desires before my own. I allowed the perception of others to dictate what I should do or be. This was a disservice. Soon as I would use the word no, not be available, or not let them control me - they'd be nowhere to be found. It was as if one no erased the thousands of times I said yes. It was as if one mistake erased hundreds of good things, I'd done. Before we go any further, what does it exactly mean to live with a purpose? Living with a purpose is another way of saying that you're living intentionally. It is a way of deliberately thinking, feeling, and doing what we want, think, feel, and do.

I learned how to place people within boundaries. I learned how to keep myself #1 no matter what. I did not get to his point overnight. It took therapy, prayer, and trial and error. What I thought my purpose was in my teens, changed with each decade that went by. It was in my thirties that I realized that my purpose was my pain. What do I mean by that? I love enriching, supporting, and inspiring folks of all ages. Specifically, young people are my favorite. The effect I've had on many of the youth I've worked with has shown that it is my pain that has made me effective. Being raw and authentic with my pain and life experiences, has made me extremely relatable. There is a level of understanding and empathy, which allows me to build connections and trust with the people I serve or interact with.

My pain and trauma is what it is. I've done my best to press on and heal from it all. Some areas I've been very successful and some I am still working to heal from. Having depression hinders me more in these situations, but that's a conversation for another day. However, every single experience sustains the effectiveness that I have with the people I serve. This is due to there being almost no area in which I cannot relate to or understand.

When going through a rough time, especially if things are traumatic or overwhelming, we can feel as if we are not going to make it. Some of us want to give up. Some of us sink into a dark place and feel as if they won't be able to come out of it, or don't know how. Many will want to give up. However, if we do the work (e.g. therapeutic, holistic, etc.). We will realize that there is not just purpose in our pain, but there is power too. Finding purpose in life is one of those things that most people want. Whether we know it or not. As nice as it sounds, it can seem challenging to attain.

If you haven't spent a lot of time thinking about your own purpose, you might have some preconceived ideas about the purpose of life. Finding your purpose in living is more than a cliché: Learning how to live your life with purpose can lead to a sense of control, satisfaction, and general contentment. Feeling like what you do is worthwhile is, arguably, a significant key to a happy life. A personal sense of purpose is less of a specific end goal and more of an ongoing impact on the world, large or small. Purpose is your why. A 2016 study published in the Journal of Research and Personality, found that individuals who feel a sense of purpose make more money than individuals who feel as though their work lacks meaning.

In 2021, the New York times, published an article where they listed 12 tips to getting started with finding your purpose and meaning in your life. Those tips are:

1.   Develop a growth mindset - Embrace challenges as opportunities.

2.   Create a personal vision statement - A purpose statement makes it easier for you to make decisions aligned to your values and helps you stay motivated as you work toward your personal goals.

3.   Give back - Look for ways to be of service. You might want to volunteer in your local community or donate your money or skills to a cause that resonates with you. Or try spreading a little happiness by performing random acts of kindness.

4.   Practice gratitude - Practicing gratitude can feel a bit awkward at first.

We get so used to our negative thoughts that switching them for positive ones can feel unnatural.

5.   Turn your pain into purpose - Many people ask for help when struggling to overcome a major life change. Some later find their purpose in helping others facing similar struggles to those they have overcome.

6.   Explore your passions - Your passions and interests are a good indicator of the area in which your life purpose might lie. If you're not sure what your passions are, ask the people who know you best.

7.   Be part of a community - Joining or creating a community allows you to find that sense of connection with others as you work together toward a common goal.

8.   Spend time with people who inspire you - Motivational speaker Jim Rohn said, "You are the average of the five people you spend the most time with." If you spend time with people who are positive and purpose-driven, they are likely to inspire you to have the same mindset.

9.   Read - Nonfiction books are useful for acquiring knowledge on certain subjects. However, research suggests that reading fiction may have more benefits. Reading fiction improves your empathy. Along with your critical and creative thinking.

10.   Join a cause - We all have a cause that we feel passionate about. Perhaps you have strong feelings about social justice, animal welfare, or the environment. Whatever it is, getting involved with a cause will help you find more purpose in your life.

11.   Practice self-acceptance - Accepting your limitations can help you be kinder to yourself when things go wrong. We all make mistakes, but instead of beating yourself up for your failures, try to see each setback as an opportunity to grow.

12.   Taking time for self-care - Self-care comes in many forms, and your version of self-care is unique to you. Perhaps you like walking in the forest, practicing some deep breathing, or journaling out your difficult emotions. You cannot achieve or serve others when you are battling against yourself.

Behind every successful person is clarity of purpose. And unless you find yours, you'll continue to cruise through life on autopilot. You may find yourself knocked off-course and lost, uncertain how to move forward or which direction is forward. Life may be smooth but one day you may look back and wish you had used your time differently. Identifying, acknowledging, and honoring your purpose is the foundation of a well-rounded life.

There are people who willingly or unwillingly live their lives based on society's dictates and preferences. I'm talking about people who are constantly living outside their purpose and are unhappy about it. While sadness is an emotion that is as common as happiness. A constant state of sadness will cause you to slip into a pattern of automatic negative thoughts, which can be more difficult to get out of.

I know firsthand that nothing else matters if you aren't following your soul's purpose. Once you've found it, you can align all areas of your life to point in that direction. It is possible to do what you love and live in flow. You just need the right motivation and mindset, and to take the right action. Once you seek, embrace, and execute your purpose; there will be a variety of benefits, that you will acquire. Margaret Olatubosun, a creative coach, states that the benefits of living with purpose are:

1. You feel grounded to a calling that is bigger than yourself.
2. You help others live their purpose by empowering them.
3. You engage with others from a point of healthy self-esteem.
4. Your physical and mental health will thank you.
5. Letting go of failure is easier.
6. Forgiving others and letting go of bitterness becomes easier.
7. Gratitude becomes an essential part of your life.
8. You engage in positive behaviors.
9. You expand your worldview.

10. You develop more empathy for others.

11. You pursue a values-based life.

12. You are more aligned with your career.

13. You gain clarity about the future despite uncertainties.

It is extremely important that you are specific about how you want to live your life and what you want it to look like. If you're breaking society's rules or following some trend, you alone are responsible for your personal fulfillment and joy. You will only get one life. Therefore, you should make it a priority to find meaning in it.

"If you can't figure out your purpose, figure out your passion. For your passion will lead you right into your purpose."

~Bishop T.D. Jakes

Every lesson not learned will be
repeated.

You got to leave people behind. Not because there was no love, but because there was no growth.

~Brittney Revere

Confidence is not 'they will like me'.
Confidence is 'I'll be fine if they don't.

Pray.
Set goals.
Make a plan.
Work hard.
Succeed.
Thank God.
Be Humble.

Live fully. The most important things in life cannot be seen but must be felt with the heart. Be kind and generous. Simplify. Have patience and compassion. Be grateful for the gifts you've been given. Challenge yourself. Inspire someone. Take the road less traveled. It's never too late.

Resilience is accepting your new reality, even if it's less good than the one you had before. You can fight it, you can do nothing but scream about what you've lost, or you can accept that and try to put together something that's good.

~Elizabeth Edwards

Hold yourself responsible for a higher
standard than anybody else expects of
you. Never excuse yourself. Never pity
yourself. Be hard master to yourself
and be lenient to everybody else.

~Henry Ward Beecher

In our personal lives, if we do not
develop our own self-awareness and
become responsible for first creations,
we empower other people and
circumstances to shape our lives by
default.

~Stephen Covey

When you reach the end of your rope,
tie a knot and hang on.

~Abraham Lincoln

I'd rather regret the risks that didn't
work out, than the chances I didn't
take at all.

~Simone Biles

Work hard in silence and let your
success be the noise.

~Frank Ocean

After getting what you manifested, ask for discipline to keep it and wisdom to multiply it.

I didn't grow up having role models. I grew up having people I didn't want to be like and seeing situations I'd never want to be in. Not all of us are dealt the right cards but that doesn't mean you can't reshuffle your deck for a better outcome.

Your storm is running out of rain.
Your challenges will end, your heart
will heal, and your soul will be at
peace again.

Your other half will either be your
better half or make you half of what
you could be. They will either inspire
you to greatness or reduce you to
mediocrity.

~Pastor Keion Henderson

If taking care of yourself means
disappointing someone else, then
disappoint them #LiveFree

~Devon Franklin

I have nothing in common with lazy
people who blame others for their lack
of success. Great things come from
hard work and perseverance. No
excuses – dedication sees dreams
come true.

~Kobe Bryant

About The Author

Ra'Mone Marquis is a southern gentleman, born and raised in the sunshine state of Florida. Life experiences and literary idols such as Omar Tyree, Terry McMillan, and Eric Jerome Dickey; have shaped Ra'Mone into the author that he is today. This is what formed the foundation of him being a refreshing literary artist with high levels of uniqueness and relatability.

Seeing a need in his community, specifically with that of minority youth, Ra'Mone started his 501c3 foundation – Tru Phoenix Foundation, Inc. (formerly known as True T.A.L.E.N.T.S. Foundation, Inc.). Since its inception, this foundation has served a plethora of minority youth in the central and south Florida areas through its mentoring conference, mentoring sessions, and various initiatives.

Courtesy of his company Tru Phoenix, LLC., formally Kace Books, LLC., he has released 7 books. They are all 5-star reviewed and 4 have reached the Amazon Bestsellers List.
They are:

1. District 69: The Crimson Edition
2. District 69: The Color Haven
3. District 69: The Greek Chronicles
4. A Poetic Exhale (his 1st #1 book)
5. Ice Box: Rebound & Recover
6. Peek A Boo: My Thoughts, My Life, My Soul
7. Pulse, Pressure, Pleasure

All books are available on Kindle, Amazon, ibooks, and his website (www.ramonemarquisofficial.com).
Ra'Mone is also the host of his own podcast, The QB Zone. All episodes are available on iheartradio, Spotify, Apple Podcasts, Google Podcasts, Audible,

and Amazon Music. Video episodes available on his
YouTube channel: QuisBox.